THE UNITED STATES
A Study of a Developing Country

Other books by Ira Sharkansky:

Spending in the American States
The Politics of Taxing and Spending
Regionalism in American Politics
The Routines of Politics
Public Administration: Policy-Making in Government Agencies
Policy Analysis in Political Science
State and Urban Politics (with Richard I. Hofferbert)
Urban Politics and Public Policy (with Robert L. Lineberry)
The Maligned States: Policy Accomplishments, Problems, and Opportunities
Policy and Politics in American Governments (with Donald S. Van Meter)

The United States

A Study of a Developing Country

Ira Sharkansky

DAVID McKAY COMPANY, INC.
New York

THE UNITED STATES:
A Study of a Developing Country

COPYRIGHT © 1975 BY David McKay Company, Inc.

ISBN: 0-679-30287-5 (paper)
0-679-50563-6 (cloth)
LIBRARY OF CONGRESS CATALOG CARD NUMBER: 75-963
MANUFACTURED IN THE UNITED STATES OF AMERICA
Design by Bob Antler

SECOND PRINTING, JANUARY 1976

Pages 79-84: Copyright © 1968, 1970, 1974 by Edward C. Banfield. From *The Unheavenly City Revisited* by Edward C. Banfield, by permission of Little, Brown and Company, Inc.

Pages 107, 109-10: From *The Gallup Poll, 1935-1971* by George Gallup. Copyright © 1972 by American Institute of Public Opinion. Reprinted by permission of Random House, Inc.

Pages 111-12: *Race in the City: Political Trust and Public Policy in the New Urban System* by Joel D. Aberbach and Jack L. Walker. Copyright © 1973 by Little, Brown and Company, Inc. Reprinted by permission.

Page 113: From Donald J. Devine, *The Political Culture of the United States: The Influence of Member Values on Regime Maintenance.* Copyright © 1972 by Little, Brown and Company, Inc. Reprinted by permission.

For Ina, Erica, and Stefan

☆ ───────────────────

PREFACE

This book grew at the borders of numerous interests. After several years writing about the American states, I sought to broaden my understanding of policy making by looking at the different context of developing countries. In preparing for a study of East Africa, I read widely in the work of economists and political scientists and began to notice several traits in the poor countries that also appear in low-income American states. Others had commented about single-party dominance in the two settings, but this took on new meaning when viewed in conjunction with other parallels that had not received much attention: the special roles of central governments in poor states and poor countries, and the prominence of regressive tax and spending policies.

Also at this time, I was reading with suspicion the description of a "postindustrial" United States, and recommendations for limiting further growth. I recalled my boyhood in Fall River, Massachusetts, a city made *postindustrial* when its industries departed, leaving the work force dependent on unemployment compensation and public assistance. The notion of a postindustrial society also seemed sharply at odds with the rural South, Appalachia, and other economic backwaters. Some time later, I began to describe three contrasts in the United States of the kind that development economists call "dualism": the regional variety between rich and poor states, intraurban dualism, and racial dualism. Each of these reveals sharp differences between more-developed and less-developed sectors, and raises serious questions about the postindustrial nature of the country and the legitimacy of a strategy to limit growth. My skeptical reading of *The Limits to Growth,* in particular, led me to doubt that we could halt growth while continuing to expand opportunities for the poor.

As this book was being readied for the press, high rates of inflation and unemployment—both records for the recent period—were producing a new awareness of economic problems. There was less talk about the security of a postindustrial society and more of a preoccupation with jobs, prices, and the adequacy of our fuel supply. This book is not written for the most current events, and it does not offer a clear path out of the country's economic problems. Yet its basic message with respect to the sectors demanding growth against those demanding simplistic conservation has great importance for the current scene.

Much poverty within the United States is not simply short-term, and seems unlikely to improve under conditions that would dampen growth. The conservation of natural amenities also requires an abundance of resources, with a gross national product that rises instead of declines. Policy makers must look beyond more tolerable indicators of prices or employment. The proper balance between growth and conservation—with more of a tilt toward growth than has been fashionable in intellectual circles—demands attention now for the long run.

In the lengthy evolution of this book, I have acquired many debts. This may be true in writing any book, but it is certainly true when exploring new and diverse concerns. For me, the past several years have offered many discoveries about a field in which I had not been trained. Critics may find weaknesses in my understanding of economic development. To many friends among political scientists and economists, however, I owe great thanks for what I have been able to learn about this complex and fascinating field.

There are many people—in universities, government, and the mass media, in the United States and abroad—who helped me greatly by their responses to my lectures and papers. To attempt to mention the most important would undoubtedly slight some because of unintentional omissions. I can give thanks to Bonnie Cleary and Linda Rau for typing; to Patrick Grasso, Barry Cline, and Stefan Sharkansky for research assistance; to the Graduate Research Committee of the University of Wisconsin–Madison for financial assistance; and to Kenneth M. Dolbeare, George J. Graham, Jr., and Aaron Wildavsky for reading the entire first draft. PUBLIUS: *The Journal of Federalism* and *Tulane Studies in Political Science* published two papers that I wrote on my way to this book.

Special thanks—and the dedication—go to Ina, Erica, and Stefan. They have suffered through my preoccupation with one project after another. If there is any merit in what I have written, it is due in part to their acceptance of my work. I owe them a great deal.

IRA SHARKANSKY
March 1975

CONTENTS

xi

THE UNITED STATES
A Study of a Developing Country

1

☆ _____

WHY WE SHOULD VIEW
THE UNITED STATES AS A
DEVELOPING COUNTRY

To say that the United States is a developing country is to
challenge much of the contemporary wisdom. Sentiments to
clean the air, save trees and wildlife, limit agribusiness, and
halt population growth have the force of dogma. Nevertheless,
the appeal to these sentiments is concentrated among the
well-to-do and better educated. In working-class neighborhoods, black ghettos, low-income states, and regional enclaves
such as Appalachia, the prevailing concerns are more jobs,
stable incomes, and increased opportunities for consumption.

The arguments of growth vs. conservation appear in many
forms. They have a role in international disputes about oil
prices and the opportunities for further economic development available to the rich and poor countries. They also appear
in countless local issues: about new power plants, flood control, and the development of industry, housing, or recreation.

A fascinating aspect of the United States is that it is both a
developed and a developing country. Great affluence lies close
to great poverty, with sharper contrasts than in any other

1

"developed" country. The diversity assures a lively dispute between those who want to keep things as they are—or roll back to a more natural state—and those who demand economic growth. Fortunately, the character of our economy permits satisfactions to both sides in the dispute. Our resources allow major efforts for the conservation of key resources and aesthetic values, plus the protection of public health and the pursuit of economic growth. We have a decent, if mixed, record in our concern for conservation as well as growth. Likewise in our willingness to transfer some of the resources produced by growth from the rich to the poor. Just as we differ from other developed countries in having extensive developing sectors, so we differ from the poor countries in being able to provide large resources for conservation and equity, as well as for growth.

Any assessment of the United States must reckon with its great diversity. Severe poverty coexists with affluence. Anyone who describes the United States as a "postindustrial society" capable of limiting growth in order to preserve amenities has not weighed the legitimate demands for more growth that come out of the poor sectors. The internal contrasts resemble those which developmental economists label "dualism" in poor countries.

Consider the cities of the United States. The rot and filth of ghettos lie within walking distance of high-rise glass and steel, just as they do in the capital cities of Africa, Asia, and Latin America. The violent crimes in our urban centers reflect social tensions and the lack of a settled character that make our cities less developed than those of most other affluent countries. Once, in preparation for a trip to India, I visited with a student from that country. He had traveled widely, and was proud to tell me of India's diverse attractions. At the end, however, he urged me to avoid Calcutta. He described sprawl, congestion, poverty, and violent crime. "It's too much like Detroit," was his summary observation.

Before clarifying the designation of the United States as a developing country, it is essential to face the bizarre nature of the issue. Why ask about the United States as a developing country? It is the most-developed nation economically. It does not possess the highest per capita income only because a sandy sheihkdom with few people has managed to ride very simple measures of average income on the escalating price of crude oil. On more complex indicators that measure the productivity of diverse economic sectors in manufacturing, services, and the production of raw materials, as well as average personal incomes, the United States is without peer. In later chapters comparative statistics document these facts, but here we can rest with the report that median family income in the United States has surpassed $12,000. This national average is higher than salaries received by such professionals as physicians and college professors in several countries thought of as "developed," and far beyond the imagination of most people in the southern continents.

Why shouldn't we pursue the more common theme of describing the American economy as overdeveloped to the point of threatening its environment through pollution or resource depletion? Why not describe the American society as "postindustrial," in the sense that it is no longer preoccupied with the production of tangible goods? Books with such titles as *The Limits to Growth* and *Population Bomb* capture the thinking of many people in the United States. And there is some truth to these fears of excessive growth, as there is to the perception that many Americans have gone beyond a preoccupation with material production. Yet these descriptions capture only part of the contemporary United States.

The contrasting sides of the United States are most evident when they are viewed geographically or socially. Much of the difference is regional; extreme instances of developed (perhaps overdeveloped) and developing sectors are separated territorially by hundreds of miles. Some of the difference divides social groups, however, and then the distances shrink to postindustrial and developing enclaves in the same metropolitan area. For many of us, "developed" and "developing" are contrasting moods that compete for our attention and loyalties. For example, we are torn between our recognition of surplus consumption and serious poverty; or we find ourselves fighting off the temptations of a job that will provide personal satisfactions with modest tangible rewards—which we would accept if operating in the postindustrial mode—with the assertion of the need to maximize income in order to provide for the family. Sometimes the features of a developed and developing society are all jumbled together. This was the case when the most affluent and sophisticated components of the United States devised analytic procedures to squeeze maximum value out of each dollar spent. Planning—programming—budgeting came out of the Defense Department in the early 1960s and was spread to state and local governments by the Ford Foundation. Its most complete version required elaborate computers and highly trained analysts; as such, it depended on the resources of a wealthy country. Yet its purpose was to economize: to produce social goals (including economic growth) with the minimum expenditure of scarce resources.

The United States is not a typical African, Asian, or Latin American country. Still, it does have enough traits in common with these areas to make the comparison worthwhile. We can learn some important things about the United States by looking at it in ways that social scientists look at the very poor countries. The effort should put into proper perspective the competing view that the United States has reached the limits of growth and should now maximize conservation instead of growth. We must recognize the strong drives for continued growth that exist within this country, appreciate the legitimacy of those drives, and plan for the satisfaction of those drives in any projections of our future.

What are the traits that liken the United States to the commonly described "developing countries"? Many of them are economic in nature; they concern the problems of our depressed regions and social classes. Landmark publications over the last fifteen years have included the books of Harry Caudill and Michael Harrington as well as Rachel Carson and Paul Ehrlich.[1] Poverty in Appalachia and other regional pockets, and in urban ghettos, provides the contrasts with national averages to highlight our own lack of uniform development. These areas of poverty justly demand further growth. They also provide us with the condition that developmental economists have labeled *dualism* in the Third World, i.e., the existence of highly developed and very backward economic and social conditions in close proximity to one another. Discussions of dualism usually depict slums adjacent to splendid homes in cities like Rio de Janeiro, Nairobi, and Bangkok, or contrast the affluent Westernized classes with illiterate country people immersed in a subsistence economy.

For the political scientist, dualism in poor countries poses the threat of such uneven rates of development as to set the stage for political unrest. The "revolution of rising expectations," whereby popular demands for benefits grow faster than the capacity of the economy to provide the rewards, draws its force from the immediate contrasts between the local poor and the local elite. It is the Mercedes of the businessman and politician, together with their swimming pools, private schools for their children, and reports of illegal payments secreted away in Switzerland that figure in the writings of left-wing

1. Harry M. Caudill, *Night Comes to the Cumberlands: A Biography of a Depressed Area* (Boston: Little, Brown, 1963); Michael Harrington, *The Other America* (Baltimore, Md.: Penguin 1962); Rachel Carson, *Silent Spring* (Boston: Houghton Mifflin, 1962); Paul R. Ehrlich, *The Population Bomb* (New York: Ballantine, 1968).

intellectuals and reflect the drives of the politically aware poor.

In the United States, a likeness to the politically charged dualism of poor countries appears in the urban ghetto. Although large-scale urban unrest has declined from the late 1960s, conflagrations in Los Angeles, Newark, and Cleveland provoked our fears of uncontrolled mobs. What features served to lessen the frequency of these outbreaks is not clear; nor do we know whether—or when—a new escalation of the violence will start.

The Nature of Economic Development

Economic development has many facets. When used by analysts, it concerns economic balance and distribution, as well as the sheer magnitude of economic resources, productivity, and growth rates. Many economists and policy makers recognize that a "developed" economy must offer rewards to a broad spectrum of the population, especially those who are (or are capable of becoming) politically organized in ways that threaten the status quo. Thus, programs defended as promoting economic development include provisions to spread the benefits of social services and job opportunities to social classes and geographic regions that are currently getting less than a fair share of the economy's rewards. Many poor countries have programs to enhance the economic opportunities of ethnic, linguistic, or regional groups that are currently on the underside of the reward structures. In the United States, affirmative action programs increase educational and job opportunities for women, blacks, American Indians, and Spanish-speaking people; and regional commissions spur economic growth in Appalachia, the Upper Great Lakes, New England, the Ozarks, coastal areas of the Carolinas and Georgia, plus the "four corners" region of Colorado, New Mexico, Arizona, and Utah.

The various components of a "developed" economy fit more or less neatly into seven categories:[2]

1. *Natural resources,* including the value of agricultural land, fuel, and minerals other than fuel
2. *Capital,* i.e., human, physical, or financial resources that can be invested in the maintenance or growth of economic potential, as measured by indices for financial assets, the skills of the population, and industrial, power, and transportation facilities
3. *Quality of industry and agriculture,* with particular attention to the use of "modern" productive technologies and schemes of organization and management, often measured by the value of products in relation to worker inputs
4. *Capacity of financial institutions* needed for public and private investments, shown by such features as the effectiveness of the tax system, central banks, commercial banking, plus stock and monetary exchanges
5. *Character of foreign trade,* with the more developed economies showing greater exports of processed and manufactured goods, as opposed to raw agricultural or mineral exports
6. *Institutions to enhance human resources,* including technological and scientific education, plus research institutes, health facilities, and programs that contribute to the economic security of the population

2. See Irma Adelman and Cynthia Taft Morris, *Society, Politics, and Economic Development* (Baltimore, Md.: Johns Hopkins University Press, 1967), chap. 2.

7. *Equality of economic opportunities and rewards,* i.e., evenness in the distribution of benefits among the various regional and social divisions of the society

This simple listing of various meanings for economic development should not hide the disputes they provoke. To some advocates, productivity in industry and agriculture is the prime target; to others, development is worth nothing without better human resources and a more equal distribution of benefits.[3] For some writers, *economic growth* refers to increases in the sheer volume of goods, services, and capital; *development* is reserved for that combination of many events that prompts upward change in most of the components noted above. For our purposes, however, it is less important to rank the components of economic development than it is to recognize that there *are* several components, and that disagreements exist among experts as to which are more and which are less central to the process of development.

The Focus on Economic Development

Scholars who deal with developing countries make a distinction between economic development and political development. *Political development* is, if possible, an even more contentious concept than economic development. To various writers, a "developed" political system means greater democracy; its components are more political competition, freedom of expression, the regular transfer of power between a government that loses to a government that wins at the polls, plus legislative and judicial branches that are capable of exercising independent scrutiny over the chief executive and the

3. See, for example, James D. Cockcroft et al., *Dependence and Underdevelopment: Latin America's Political Economy* (Garden City, N.Y.: Anchor, 1972).

bureaucracy.[4] To critics of this perspective, however, the equation of *democracy* with *political development* is a cultural bias rooted in British, North American, or Western European origins. A contrasting view sees a developed political system as one that is stable and reasonably predictable in its transitions from one government to another, no matter how the governing elites are chosen or how they exercise their power.

It is not the intention of this book to become absorbed in disputes about the nature of political development. Our use of the word *development* is in its economic context. We spend a great deal of time discussing the various political arrangements that appear at different levels of (economic) development, but there is no intention of asserting any position with respect to the meaning of political development.

Political Features Associated with Less-Developed Economies

Less-developed sectors of the American economy resemble less-developed countries in certain political traits. American states with the least-developed economies depend heavily on "foreign" sources of financial capital and political leadership. There is little party competition over state offices. State chief executives tend to be powerful figures in the policy-making process with little significant opposition from the legislative branch of state government. State governments have also acquired great power at the expense of local authorities in the poor states, a situation that resembles the centralization of power at the national level in most poor countries. The tax levies in these states tend to be regressive; they rely heavily on

4. See Samuel P. Huntington, *Political Order in Changing Societies* (New Haven: Yale University Press, 1968); and Seymour Martin Lipset, *Political Man* (Garden City, N.Y.: Doubleday, 1960), chap. 2.

general sales taxes, which take their biggest bites out of low incomes. And the budgets of these states are not generous in their programs for the poor.

The political similarities between less-developed states and less-developed countries are not simply coincidental but serve to support certain strategies for pursuing economic growth that the less-developed states and countries also share.

Centralization of government, strong chief executives, and limited party competition serve to limit the number of people with influence over public policy. Most often the excluded are the poor who would—if they could—demand social programs for their own needs. Yet the taxes of poor states and poor countries place their heaviest burdens on the lowest-income class; these taxes offer large allocations for programs which provide their most immediate payoff to the middle- and upper-income classes—e.g., highways, the development of natural resources, and subsidies for industry. Depending on one's perspective, such strategies can promise great benefits for the mass of the population over the long run; or they are a ripoff of the poor to benefit the rich, with scant prospect of benefits trickling down to the masses.

The American Peculiarity

Some readers may have begun this book with the image of a developing country set in an exotic climate and populated by dark-skinned people at abject levels of poverty. At this point they may be receptive to the view of the United States as "developing," at least in certain respects. Yet, they may ask, if the United States is a developing country, then aren't all countries "developing"? If the answer to this question is yes, then the concept of a developing country is useless: it no longer distinguishes among countries or permits further analysis as to those characteristics that follow from being a "developing" country.

It is tempting to believe that "if the United States is a developing country, then all of them must be" because the United States is so well developed in certain economic traits. As we have seen, however, economic development has several dimensions, and on one item—equality of opportunities and benefits—the United States scores lower than other countries that are highly developed in terms of sheer wealth. Unlike Canada, Australia, New Zealand, Japan, and the other countries of Western Europe, the United States has a sizable portion of its population at a standard of living substantially below the national average. This is not to say that other highly developed countries have no problems of distribution. They do. Canada has the Maritimes, rural Quebec, and its far north; Australia, its aborigines; Scandinavian countries, their rural north; and all countries have regional enclaves of poverty. But none of the highly developed countries has the regional and the social inequalities of the United States, affecting such a large percentage of the population, and with the disadvantaged population so strategically placed with respect to the centers of national economic and political life. Look at blacks in the United States, by way of example: 11 percent of the total population are increasingly concentrated in urban areas where the confluence of poverty, poor housing, crime, discrimination, inadequate education, and sophisticated job requirements create a tangled morass and political tinder.

The eleven states of the former Confederacy provide another illustration of an economic enclave. Impressive pockets of affluence in Florida, Texas, and Virginia seem to belie the image of "underdeveloped," but this region remains one of lower-than-average income and traditional politics. The American South is still the most distinctive region on a host of economic, social, and political traits. Its importance is meas-

ured by its 25 percent of the national population, 22 percent of
the United States Senate, 25 percent of the seats in the House
of Representatives, and 24 percent of the electoral college.
Political leaders in the South, like leaders of the black community and other low-income ethnic groups, seek economic
growth. Theirs is not the rhetoric of postindustrial society or
limited growth; they speak of more economic development,
and as rapidly as possible, to provide more tangible benefits for
their people.

Implications of Viewing the United States as a Developing Country

The United States is a developing country not simply because
it includes poor people and poor regions, whose leaders pursue
strategies of economic growth. The designation comes because
of these traits and because of political parallels that exist
between the less-developed sectors of the United States and
the less-developed countries of the world. The number of these
parallels shows the depth of the similarities and suggests the
deep roots of the demands for growth.

Implications for the United States

The most profound implication of this finding is the need
to qualify the widespread and often persuasive writings on the
theme of the United States as a postindustrial or overdeveloped country that should maximize values of conservation ahead of growth.[5]

Not too long ago, growth was an unchallenged goal of
American businessmen and public officials. More was better: in
the scale of production, size of markets, and personal incomes.

5. For example, Donella H. Meadows et al., *The Limits to Growth* (New
York: Universe, 1972).

For state and local governments, more people meant more tax revenues and a larger base of demand on which to project growth rates for highways, schools, parks, and social workers. Now we are several years into a concern with too much growth, and its by-products of crowding, pollution, and resource depletion. In the swing from boosting growth to seeing virtues in stability, however, we have lost sight of the merits of growth. Some boosters remain, seeing in growth more of a panacea than a threat. But there is much confusion, and no shortage of conflict.

Any projection of our near-term future must count on continued tensions between demands of growth and demands of environmental protection. The tensions between the less-developed and postindustrial sectors within the United States will produce continued diversity in policy goals: pursuit of industrial growth despite pollution in some places vs. an emphasis on clear air and water elsewhere. At the national level, clashes will take place between those who would maximize environmental values at any price, and those who would insist on treating the environment as a calculable value with limited worth. Those who see growth as less urgent will speak most often for preservation of the environment.

Kentucky has more than its share of internal contrasts. There is poverty in the eastern mountains, a healthy urban economy in Louisville, and pastoral wealth on the horse farms near Lexington. Symptomatic of these tensions is a proposal coming out of the Kentucky legislature. It seeks a state environmental and economic development policy that will focus on the conflicts between development and protection:

> Near anarchy would best describe the state of affairs that presently exist in the area of conflict between economic development and environmental protection. . . .
> Nobody would argue against the need for controls any

more than they would argue against the benefits we
derive from economic expansion and development, but
because the situation affects us all, everybody is getting
into the act. Although it is possible to loosely group
individuals and organizations according to their prime
bias, it is quite apparent that the diversity of values and
views held by each camp are so disparate as to prevent
agreement within the ranks let alone bridge the gap
between the camps.[6]

There is some evidence of class division over the growth
vs. conservation issue. Many of the poor, whites and blacks, are
unconvinced of their self-interest in the cause of environmental protection. Low-income states tend to promote growth,
upper-income states are more concerned with conservation.
Similar divisions occurred among nations at the 1972 United
Nations meeting in Stockholm. Representatives of the advanced Western nations spoke in favor of protecting the
world's resources from overuse; spokesmen for the poor nations saw in a policy of environmental protection a danger to
their own interests, as they strove to use their natural resources
for the pursuit of rapid economic growth. Yet, different economic interests remain only one source of policy dispute.
Growth vs. conservation combines features of economic
self-interest with ideology. Some people believe passionately
in growth or in protection, seemingly indifferent to the positions dictated by their own economic interests.

The debate between advocates of growth and advocates of
conservation is not a simple one. The different positions include strong moral assertions plus claims about the availability
of various resources and the threats posed by pollution. Each

6. "Needed: A Kentucky Environmental and Economic Development
Policy" (Kentucky Legislative Research Commission, Frankfort, 1973), p. 3.
Mimeographed.

side makes claims about the results of their strategy for the equity of economic distributions. According to those who emphasize conservation, greater equality will flow from a change toward the more public-minded values associated with the conservation ethos. To those who would maximize growth, such thinking is pie in the sky; it assumes an altruism that is unlikely in the United States. They say that, short of a political upheaval (unexpected) that would provide massive transfers of resources directly from the haves to the have-nots, benefits to the poor accrue when the total size of the economic pie is growing, thus allowing the poor—as well as the rich—to get more.

Empirical evidence does not guarantee equality more readily from a strategy of growth or one of conservation. Nevertheless, the edge goes to the side saying that growth produces more equality, at least in the long run. Economic growth provides more jobs at all levels of skills and facilitates the financial support of public services to provide basic education, job training, health care, and at least minimum income security for the aged, disabled, and unemployed. Among countries of the world as among the American states, it is the most developed (as measured by average income) that offer the most generous social services and whose residents show the greatest equality of income.[7]

Admittedly, there is considerable uncertainty about the determinants of economic equality. This is not the time to waste resources on the simple proposition that growth produces greater equality, and to use this expectation to ignore conservation demands. Indeed, it is premature to conclude that the values of growth and those of conservation are in-

7. Thomas R. Dye, "Income Inequality and American State Politics," *American Political Science Review* 63 (March 1969): 157-62; and Simon Kuznets, *Modern Economic Growth: Rate, Structure, and Spread* (New Haven: Yale University Press, 1966), especially chap. 4.

compatible. Quite the contrary. The appearance of the most sophisticated efforts at environmental preservation in the most advanced economies suggests that, strange as it may seem, a strategy of growth may be a prerequisite to conservation. In considering the United States as a *developing* country, we should not forget that it is also a *developed* country. Uniquely it possesses the needs and the resources to pursue production growth, a more equal distribution of rewards, and the conservation of key resources.

Implications for the Poor Countries

Although the focus of this book is on the United States, with insights borrowed from the experiences of poor countries, some implications go the other way, i.e., from an analysis of the United States to the experiences of poor countries. Some conclusions about the competition between different American sectors for further growth, conservation, and equality have meaning for the competitions between countries of the world for their own national goals of growth, conservation, and equality.

Within the United States, the coincidence of great wealth and poverty offers some promise for our less-developed sectors. It would be foolhardy to predict the disappearance of poverty from this country, but it is consistent with our recent history to project a continued narrowing of the gap between rich and poor. This has occurred in incomes as well as in a range of social-welfare benefits that accrue from higher incomes: better housing, educational opportunities, and medical care. Here we have established legal and political structures that serve to transfer resources from richer to poorer sectors. Much pulling and hauling may go on between groups having different interests; some are very much in favor of redistribution and some are very much opposed. The trend toward more

equal distributions has been slow, and at times it has shown
temporary reverses. Overall, our poor are relatively less poor
now than in the past. We have used our national resources at
least partly for the poor.

Can we expect the same trend toward a more equal distribution of resources between rich and poor countries? This
question introduces a profound series of issues. Standing in the
way of any international distribution of resources are problems
that do not intrude in the simpler setting of the United States.
Poor nations have no standing with respect to the wealth of
rich nations equivalent to the standing of poor citizens with
respect to the wealth of their own country. Emotional ties of
common citizenship and the more tangible clout of poor voters
in democratic politics do not apply to the relations among
nations. Poor nations can call on humanitarian virtues or cast
their votes for the emotional (but seldom tangible) issues that
appear on the agenda of the United Nations. But rich nations
are more sovereign in the control of their own resources than
are rich citizens within a democratic country. Not only is there
no effective system of international taxation, but the combination of altruism and political self-interest that serves as the
base of international assistance is volatile and recently seems
pointed away from poor countries. Foreign-aid programs of
the United States and other wealthy countries have declined as
a percentage of the donors' gross national product. Also, the
unilaterally increased price of petroleum seems likely to weigh
especially heavy on the poorest countries. Moreover, economic
gaps between rich countries and poor countries are greater
than those between rich and poor sectors within the United
States. All of this suggests a dim prospect for the continued
poverty of poor countries. Pessimism comes even in the absence of a world view that sees active conspiracies in rich
countries to exploit the poor.

Outline of This Book

The various chapters of this book detail the issues introduced here. Chapter 2 asks, "How developed is the United States?" and shows its dimensions of economic development compared with other countries; it also looks within the United States and documents some of the more striking contrasts between our more-developed and less-developed sectors. Chapters 3 through 5 look at three kinds of contrasts: between more-developed and less-developed states; metropolitan contrasts that appear within our major urban areas; and racial contrasts that make the United States different from other highly developed countries. Chapter 6 takes direct aim at the issues of economic growth, conservation, and equality; it seeks to determine if growth is a threat to society or an engine to equality and social progress. Chapter 7 asks if any prescriptions for policy makers flow from the analyses in the preceding material, and if the analysis focused on differences between developing and developed sectors of the United States has significance for the gaps between rich and poor countries of the world. Overall, it is necessary to warn the reader: this book is more strategic than tactical, and it focuses more directly on the United States than elsewhere. It seeks to show the depth and legitimacy of the growth perspective in the United States, while leaving to others the more difficult task of balancing the demands for growth with the proper concern for conservation.

2

☆

HOW DEVELOPED IS
THE UNITED STATES

For many of the world's people, the United States has long
stood as the epitome of economic opportunity. European
peasants flocked to our cities in the nineteenth century, most of
them seeking to improve themselves economically. Although
much of the capital that financed our westward expansion
came from Europe, some immigrants really did expect to find
the streets of America paved with gold.[1] After 1849, California
became a magnet for migrants both from Europe and from
within the United States; even today, California stands as the
height of American development. If any state meets the criteria
for a postindustrial society, it is probably California. It ranks
at or near the top of all the states on indicators for total population, personal income, the importance of service industries in its
economy, and the quality of its public education. The University of California serves as a model of higher education, and its
Berkeley campus scores above Harvard on at least one meas-

1. See Oscar Handlin, *The Uprooted* (Boston: Atlantic, Little, Brown,
1951).

ure of excellence in graduate education.[2] Los Angeles typifies the highly mobile, casual life style of the avant garde middle class. Professionals in public welfare, corrections, mental health, and conservation have gained for the state government a reputation for leadership in public service. California has also led in the sore spots that appear on the frontier of modernization: it spawned the most extensive suburban sprawl cum freeways; the first ghetto riot of the 1960s was in Watts; and Berkeley is a center of campus unrest, political radicalism, and terrorism.

In order to determine how developed the United States is, we must look beyond California. Another side of our country appears in Mississippi, Arkansas, West Virginia, and eastern Kentucky. Economies there are crudely industrial and preindustrial. Industries are labor-intensive, and numerous residents scratch a living from subsistence agriculture. A drive through the countryside of these regions reveals wooden shacks innocent of exterior paint, window glass, or interior plumbing. These areas' vital statistics show high levels of infant mortality. The armed services reject a disproportionate number of recruits from these states for failure to pass the mental examination. Harry Caudill probes the background of eastern Kentucky in *Night Comes to the Cumberlands*[3] and finds cultural faults that go back to the first settlers. Indentured servants who had come originally from British slums escaped from eastern Carolina and Virgina; they and their descendants were isolated from the currents that developed outside Appalachia in the nineteenth and twentieth centuries.

Is California or the rural South more typical of the United States? Because of the size and diversity of this country, the

2. Kenneth D. Roose and Charles J. Andersen, *A Rating of Graduate Programs* (Washington, D.C.: American Council on Education, 1970), as presented in Ira Sharkansky, *The Maligned States: Policy Accomplishments, Problems, and Opportunities* (New York: McGraw-Hill, 1972), p. 93.

3. Boston: Little, Brown, 1963.

answer is, "Neither." Other, better questions will give answers
that show various sides of the American setting. In some features the country as a whole is highly developed; but in other
features it lags behind Canada, Australia, and much of Europe. And there is more complexity here than can be shown by
the simple extremes of California and the rural South. In order
to delineate those attributes of the United States that are important to this book, let us first compare the country as a whole
with other countries on several economic and social dimensions. Then we can look within the United States to determine
which parts of the country are more, and less, developed.

Postindustrial Society

The idea of a postindustrial society is useful when evaluating
the United States. The concept has passed widely among social
commentators. It provides a starting point for numerous rat-
ings of contemporary affairs and for projections of trends into
the future. Since the term has become popular, it has been
subject to various definitions and some modification (e.g.,
"mature industrial" and "advanced industrial" society). Yet its
various meanings cluster around those provided by Daniel Bell
when he popularized the concept in 1967.

The key features of a postindustrial society are an economy dominated by the service sector and a high incidence of
sophisticated technology; rapid changes in products, services,
and social institutions; a major role for government in the
provisions of social benefits; and a leadership comprised of
individuals and institutions at the forefront of technological
change. In Bell's words,

> We can begin with the fact that ours is no longer
> primarily a manufacturing economy. The service sector

(comprising trade; finance, insurance and real estate; personal, professional, business, and repair services; and general government) now accounts for more than half of the total employment and more than half of the gross national product. . . . The ganglion of the post-industrial society is knowledge. . . . In all this, the university, which is the place where theoretical knowledge is sought, tested, and codified in a disinterested way, becomes the primary institution of the new society. Perhaps it is not too much to say that if the business firm was the key institution of the past hundred years, because of its role in organizing production for the mass creation of products, the university will become the central institution of the next hundred years because of its role as the new source of innovation and knowledge.[4]

The postindustrial society seems to be the high point of social and economic evolution. Bell is careful to note that such a society has its conflicts over questions of distribution that cannot be settled by technology alone. Yet he and his followers indicate that the productive capacity of a postindustrial society provides the resources to accommodate diverse interests. Also, sophisticated modes of analysis with sensitive social indicators aid in problem solving. The role of government increases to accommodate the demands of groups that are economically insecure: blacks, farmers, and blue-collar workers. These groups seek government protection from the problems they encounter in the marketplace. A productive economy can provide the resources needed to meet their demands, and the government of a postindustrial society can identify these resources and assemble them from the economy. Bell points to

4. Daniel Bell, *The Coming of Post-Industrial Society: A Venture in Social Forecasting* (New York: Basic, 1973). This quotation is taken from the earlier "Notes on the Post-Industrial Society," *Public Interest* (Winter and Spring 1967).

the cold war and the space race as two events that put the American government in a "mobilized posture," i.e., capable of extracting great resources from the economy to be used for public purposes. In order to meet the postindustrial criteria, a society should exhibit high standards of living distributed widely throughout its population; sophisticated programs to assure its people of benefits in the fields of education, health, and housing; and a work force that is engaged more in the production of services to one another than in manufacturing.

Writing in 1967, Daniel Bell felt that the United States was postindustrial, or at least as close to being so as any other major society. This assessment has certain implications for further development. If the United States is a postindustrial society, the future would be less one of further growth than of concern for the conservation of as-yet-untapped resources and for cleaning the environment.

Daniel Bell provides extensive illustrations of a postindustrial society, but his documentation typically shows aggregates for the country as a whole and does not illuminate its internal contrasts. Further, his theory does not always lend itself to precise definition in terms that match the economic and social indicators available about the United States or other countries. In the pages that follow, some inferences must be made about complex social and economic conditions from simple indicators. This is frequently the plight of the social scientist. The information available does not always fit neatly into the categories required by the analysis. Here we are interested in comparing the United States with other countries on several dimensions of internal homogeneity, to see how they fit the postindustrial model. As we quarrel with Bell's designation of the United States as a postindustrial society, it will be possible for others to quarrel with our designation of the United States as a developing country. In both cases, the argument should not turn over the interpretation of a particular statistic, but over the accumulated weight of all the argument and evidence.

The United States in International Comparisons

On aggregate measures of economic resources and industrial magnitude, the United States stands above all other countries as the most developed country in the world. When it comes to measurements of social conditions, however, including the distribution of income and the quality of health, housing, and popular literacy, this country surrenders its leadership position. And by looking at various regions within the United States, it is possible to find conditions that bear closer resemblance to the poor countries of Africa, Asia, and Latin America than to the more developed areas of Western Europe and North America.

The United States has no equal among sizable countries on such measures of sheer economic muscle as gross domestic product per capita and energy consumption per capita. The United States scores higher on these indicators than any country of Western Europe, and towers over the poorest countries of Africa, Asia, and Latin America. The United States has over seventy times the per capita gross domestic product of Ethiopia and almost four hundred times the per capita energy consumption of Haiti! We also eat more (in terms of average calories per day) than any other country except Ireland; Americans eat almost twice as much as Indonesians and Bolivians.[5]

When we turn to a common measure of income distribution, however, the United States surrenders its lead to countries with more egalitarian cultures and tax systems. The Gini

5. Unless indicated otherwise, the data showing national aggregates come from *Statistical Abstract of the United States, 1972* and *1973* (Washington, D.C.: U.S. Government Printing Office, 1973 and 1974).

coefficient, named after the Italian statistician who devised it, measures the way in which certain traits (in this case, incomes) are distributed in a population. Its computation reflects the amount of total income available to each income segment of the population. For example, if the poorest 25 percent of a population has only 5 percent of the total income in the country, that country has a less equal distribution of incomes than if the poorest 25 percent of the population had 10 percent of the total income. Perfect equality would exist if each percentage of the population had the matching percentage of total income: the bottom 1 percent had 1 percent of the income; the bottom 10 percent had 10 percent of the income; the bottom 25 percent had 25 percent of the income; and the top 1 percent had only 1 percent of the income. If this theoretical ideal prevailed, the Gini coefficient would be 0.000. The size of the Gini coefficient increases in size as the incomes become more skewed, and when each percentage of the population has—at the bottom—less than its equivalent percentages of the total income and—at the top—more than its equivalent percentage of the total income.

In a series of computations made in the 1960s, the United States scored below seven other countries in equality of income distribution. All seven countries were on the "more developed" side of the global economic spectrum, but none of them scored as high as the United States on measures of sheer resources. More equal in income distributions than the United States were the United Kingdom, Sweden, Israel, Australia, Netherlands, Luxembourg, and Belgium. For the forty-three countries whose recorded information showed them to be less equal in incomes than the United States, the prevailing pattern was a low score on most measures of economic development.[6] This finding is reconsidered in a later chapter, i.e., that equality

6. Charles Lewis Taylor and Michael C. Hudson, *World Handbook of Political and Social Indicators* (2nd ed.; New Haven: Yale University Press, 1972), pp. 263–64.

of economic distribution accords with high scores on measures of sheer resources.

The United States also shows income differentials internally—among its geographical enclaves—that are more highly skewed than those of other wealthy countries. To be sure, it is not easy to compare one country with another on the topic of internal differences. The areas for which national governments collect statistics vary widely in size and homogeneity. Nevertheless, gauging the spreads between high- and low-income *provinces* in eight European countries and *counties* in the United States, the differential between wealthy and poor areas in the United States reaches a magnitude of 7.4 times; for each of the other countries, it is between 1.5 and 3.8 times.[7]

The United States is also not the first among nations on common indicators of social benefits. Admittedly, some social benefits are difficult to measure with the information available for numerous countries. For health benefits, we rely on the availability of "physicians" and rates of infant mortality. The U.S. record of infant mortality is less desirable than that of ten countries in Europe, plus Canada, Australia, New Zealand, Japan, and Taiwan. The people of fourteen countries enjoy a higher incidence of physicians in the population, including such "less developed" countries as Argentina, Bulgaria, Greece, Hungary, Poland, and the USSR. In some of these countries a person may qualify as a physician with less training than is possible in the United States. In certain American states, paramedics are legally entitled to perform services that require the attendance of physicians elsewhere. The point remains, however, that Americans encounter relatively fewer people who are legally capable of providing important varie-

---

7. John H. Chandler, "An International Comparison," *Monthly Labour Review* (1969): 55. The European countries that show less internal diversity than the United States are Belgium, Denmark, France, Germany, Italy, Netherlands, Sweden, and the United Kingdom.

ties of health care than do people in many other countries. On a widely used measure of housing quality (the percentage of dwellings with piped-in water), the United States falls below seven European countries, plus New Zealand, Israel, Canada, and Japan. If we can rate the incidence of popular literacy by the circulation of newspapers relative to population (a common measurement in international comparisons), the United States scores lower than fourteen countries.

Economic and Social Contrasts within the United States

Unfortunately, few measures directly related to the concept of a postindustrial society permit comparisons between countries. By looking at internal differences within the United States, it is possible to use more such indicators, and to be more confident that we are measuring the same phenomena from one locale to another. As we see the depth of internal differences—especially those associated with region and with race—we will encounter those traits of the American society that lower its aggregate scores on social indicators below the points expected on the basis of total resources.

It is more accurate to speak about pockets of postindustrial society within the United States than about a postindustrial United States. On a measure of the service sector in state economies, Hawaii scores more than three times as postindustrial as Mississippi;[8] Utah's incidence of college students is about three times that of South Carolina; and New

8. Hawaii's service establishments recorded receipts of $404 per capita during 1967, while Mississippi's recorded only $126, as reported in *County and City Data Book, 1972* (Washington, D.C.: U.S. Government Printing Office, 1973). Other data in this section also come from the *County and City Data Book, 1972,* or from *Statistical Abstract of the United States, 1972* and *1973* (Washington, D.C.: U.S. Government Printing Office, 1973 and 1974).

York's expenditures for elementary and secondary education are almost three times greater than Alabama's on a per-pupil basis. The simple measure of income per capita shows almost twice the resources in Connecticut as in Mississippi. A measure of infant mortality that compares races as well as states shows a rate for whites in Hawaii that is 3.5 times more desirable than that for nonwhites in Wyoming. Housing statistics show an incidence of quality in California (as measured by the proportion of dwellings with all the standard plumbing facilities) some 20 percent higher than in Mississippi.

By looking within the states at smaller units, it is possible to find even sharper differences. Fairfield County is the highest-income county in the highest-income state, Connecticut; and Jefferson County is the lowest-income county in the lowest-income state, Mississippi. These are not the extreme counties of the country in individual measurements, but they provide a convenient pairing to show many of the sharp differences that exist.

Fairfield County includes the affluent outer suburbs of New York City as well as some prosperous industrial cities that have spawned their own suburbs. The most recent government compendium of city and county statistics shows that Fairfield County's median family income in 1969 was $13,074, putting it 36 percent above the national average. Almost all its residents (92 percent) were white, and the typical adult had more than a high school education. About one-fifth of the adults had graduated from college, and less than 4 percent fell in the group with the lowest educational attainment (less than five years of school). Only 3 percent were listed as unemployed when the national average was 4.4 percent, and less than 5 percent were below the "low-income" level defined by the national government. Almost all the dwellings had the customary plumbing facilities. Those residents unfortunate enough to be on welfare received grants that averaged $259 for the program to aid families with dependent children (at a time when the national average for that program was $190).

Jefferson County is much different. On some indicators it appears closer to a preindustrial than a postindustrial model. Located along the Mississippi River, some 90 miles southwest of Jackson, its social indicators showed a poor, black, un-educated population with housing facilities that resemble those of poor countries. Less than 4 percent of Jefferson County's adults had a college degree, and 59 percent had incomes below the low-income level. Blacks comprised 75 percent of the county population, and their median family income in 1969 was $2,250; this was less than one-sixth that of white families in Fairfield County, Connecticut. Almost three-quarters of the blacks' dwellings in Jefferson County lacked some plumbing facilities; this put their housing roughly on a par with that in Sri Lanka (Ceylon) and Honduras. The unemployment rate was almost 12 percent when Fairfield County's was about 3 percent, and average payments for families with dependent children in Jefferson County were only $55 per month, about one-fifth that of Fairfield County.

The coal counties of Appalachia provide one of the most vivid demonstrations of social and economic indicators that are far short of "postindustrial" in the United States. These counties captured the attention of Senator John F. Kennedy during his crucial West Virginia presidential-primary contest against Senator Hubert Humphrey in 1960. Partly because of this experience, Appalachia became the most prominent site of the regional development commissions that sprouted during the Kennedy-Johnson years. Moreover, the eastern Kentucky segment of Appalachia sired Harry Caudill, whose *Night Comes to the Cumberlands* provides one of the best portraits of an American backwater. Caudill describes the first white settlers:

... for many decades there flowed from Merry England
to the piney coasts of Georgia, Virginia and the
Carolinas a raggle-taggle of humanity—penniless
workmen fleeing from the ever-present threat of military
conscription; honest men who could not pay their debts,
pickpockets and thieves who were worth more to the
Crown on a New World plantation than dangling from a
rope, and children of all ages and both sexes, whose only
offense was that they were orphans and without
guardians capable of their care.[9]

Once over the mountains, the first Kentuckians were isolated
from Western civilization. Their agricultural background was
meager to nonexistent, having come mostly from urban slums,
and they were generally without skilled trades. They crossed
the mountains as individuals, without the institutions of an
organized church or preselected community leaders that accompanied other migrations across America.

Consider then these forces in synopsis: The illiterate son
of illiterate ancestors, cast loose in an immense
wilderness without basic mechanical or agricultural
skills, without the refining, comforting and disciplining
influence of an organized religious order, in a vast land
wholly unrestrained by social organization of effective
laws, compelled to acquire skills quickly in order to
survive, and with a Stone Age savage as his principal
teacher. From these forces emerged the mountaineer as
he is to an astonishing degree even today.[10]

What followed from these inauspicious beginnings? According to Caudill, a lack of sophistication led residents to sell

9. Caudill, *Night Comes to the Cumberlands,* p. 5.
10. Ibid., p. 31.

valuable timber and mineral rights for meager sums, lacking
due protection from companies that could exploit the resources without regard for water quality or land erosion; a lack
of concern for their own futures inhibited the development of
education and other public services and made the residents
easy prey to political as well as economic exploitation by the
coal companies. The history of eastern Kentucky (and much of
Appalachia elsewhere) has featured paternalistic company
towns and county political machines that nurture popular
dependence on short-sighted and self-interested community
leaders. This is also the land of the family feuds, many of which
began when the region was torn in its loyalties between North
and South during the Civil War and then spurted upward
again during efforts to organize mineworkers in the 1930s.
Violence was rampant; one study of Rowan County in the
1880s showed twenty "open murders and secret assassina-
tions" without a single conviction being obtained in the courts;
sixteen other people were wounded in shootings. All this in a
county of only 6,129 population and some twenty years after
the Civil War! Caudill's chapters convey the mood of his book:
"Our Disinherited Forbears," "The Wars," "The Big Bosses,"
"The Big Boom," "Moonshine and Mayhem," "From Bust to
Boom Again," "The Rape of the Appalachians," "The Politics
of Decay."

The plight of Appalachia did not pass with the end of the
Great Depression or with John Kennedy's discovery of its
poverty in 1960. Its record is one of continuing boom and bust.
The periodic booms after 1960 and most recently in 1974–75
have rewarded those miners with the training to operate sophisticated equipment, but have made the miners vulnerable
to price changes in coal or its competitive fuels, and to rulings
that constrain the use of polluting coal. The strip mine is the
latest attack on the landscape, with a cruel irony inherent in the
use of stripping to gather coal for the Tennessee Valley Au-

thority. The TVA seeks to maximize efficient production of electric power by way of cheap coal, even though it leads TVA to foster the despoilation of land and water resources in eastern Kentucky of a kind that the Authority was designed to prevent in its own region. Harlan County is representative of eastern Kentucky. Coal is the base of its economy, and its economic and social traits suffer by comparison with those of the state and nation. The average adult in Harlan County had only 8.4 years of schooling, according to recent government figures; family income levels were 63 percent of those in the state and 49 percent of those in the nation; the incidence of housing without plumbing facilities was about twice that elsewhere in Kentucky and almost seven times that in the United States; and there was a net out-migration of 37 percent between 1960 and 1970.

Georgia illustrates several varieties of more-developed and less-developed regions that occur throughout the United States. As a whole, Georgia is a typical southern state. Its aggregate figures indicate below-average scores on urbanism, a population that is thin on "foreign stock" but with heavy representation of blacks, low level of education and income, poor housing quality, and political conservatism. In the presidential election of 1968, Georgia was one of the states that gave a plurality to George Wallace's American Independent party, just as it was one of six states that voted for Barry Goldwater in 1964. Within Georgia, however, the varieties of economic development include dynamic growth in the Atlanta area, which has since World War II become a regional center for manufacturing, commerce, finance, and government. Major plants of Lockheed and the big three of the automobile industry are in the Atlanta area. Huge regional breweries of national and international brands now compete with moonshiners, and there are athletic teams in the big leagues of several professional sports. Data for suburban DeKalb County show the effects of a dynamic, wealthy economy. Median family income is 49 percent above the state average and 27 percent above the national average; DeKalb ranks forty-sixth among U.S. counties. The population is disproportionately young, white, well educated, and Republican. There is only a tiny portion of inadequate housing, and the rate of in-migration over the 1960–70 period was 42 percent—some twenty times the national average.

Much different from metropolitan Atlanta is Georgia's black belt, a broad swatch of counties extending across the middle and southern part of the state. This region is agricultural and black, rich in its productivity but poor in the incomes and living standards of its people. This is the historic land of cotton, and now the terrain of peaches, timber, beef, and a variety of other crops, plus a smattering of military bases. The long and simultaneous tenures of Richard Russell and Carl Vinson as chairmen of the Senate and House Armed Services Committees served their state well. It was often said that the state would sink with the addition of one more military establishment. But this thesis seemed to have been proved wrong by the location of the U.S. Navy Supply School in Athens, more than 200 miles from the sea but less than 40 miles from Senator Russell's home town of Winder.

Clay County is typical of Georgia's black belt. Located in the southwestern part of the state along the Alabama line, it is due west of Albany. Its 1970 population was a meager 3,636, more than 60 percent of it black. There was a 26 percent rate of out-migration in the preceding decade, and the remaining population was disproportionately old, poor, uneducated, and badly housed. With all these traits seeming to call for an active public sector, however, the voting record of the county was

conservative. Its plurality in the 1968 presidential election
went to George Wallace, reflecting the much greater participation of whites than blacks in public affairs.

Union County presents another side to the less-developed
sectors in Georgia. Some 200 miles north of Clay County, and
lying along the border with North Carolina, the name itself
says something of its history. Union is one of the mountain
counties, always empty of blacks and isolated from just about
every phase of the state's economic history. The folks up there
saw no merit in secession during the 1860s; they sided with the
Union then and have voted Republican almost uniformly
since. Leaving race aside, however, many characteristics of
Union County today look very much like those of Clay
County: a scattered rural population, out-migration, a sizable
contingent of elderly, low incomes, poor education, and
substandard housing.

Angoon Division in Alaska demonstrates that blacks do
not present the only case of extreme deprivation in the United
States. This area is in southeastern Alaska on the narrow stem
that attaches to Canada's western border. Directly south of the
state capital at Juneau, Angoon has a tiny population of 463,
only 11 percent of which is white. By one measure it is the
poorest unit in the United States. Median family income was
only $2,154 in 1969, one-fourth the national average and
one-seventh that of Montgomery County in Maryland. Over
97 percent of the families had incomes below the poverty line
that year, and no one earned more than $25,000. Over 90
percent of the homes lacked some common plumbing facility,
and the rate of unemployment was more than three times the
national average.

Fall River, Massachusetts, illustrates a cruel variety of

postindustrial society: its industrial development reached its peak in the years before World War I, and it has been downhill ever since. Population declined from 120,495 in 1920 to 96,931 in 1970. Once the most productive center of cotton textiles in the world, Fall River is now less productive in that field than any one of a dozen towns in Georgia and the Carolinas which attracted Fall River's mill owners from the turn of this century onward. Fall River is by no means the only long-depressed industrial city of New England, but it is one of the most striking in the depth of its depression and in its failure to recover through a shift to other kinds of economic activity.

During its growth in the latter part of the nineteenth century, Fall River's mill owners recruited immigrants from a half dozen European countries and French Canada. The population remains heavily ethnic. Almost 50 percent are labeled "foreign stock" by the Census Bureau, with Portuguese the largest group. Fall River's history during this century has, like that of Appalachia, featured periods of decline, bust, and occasional boom. The textile industry's departure began shortly before World War I, as southern locales offered low wages, cheap transportation close to sources of supply, modern plants, and tax concessions. The decline was slowed by the war, but then began again afterward, putting Fall River into a Great Depression some ten years before the rest of the country. World War II, Korea, and Vietnam provided later interludes in the prevailing situation of decline or stagnation. By the time of the Vietnam boomlet, the textile manufacturers had completely disappeared and their place had been taken by small clothing manufacturers, making use of the old granite mill buildings and the large supply of inexpensive, semiskilled female labor. There was a brief period of full employment in the late 1960s when immigration from Portugal increased sharply, the local schools revitalized dormant programs to teach English as a second language to schoolchildren and —also reminiscent of the old days—a local hospital reestablished its tuberculosis ward.

The greatest economic event in Fall River's recent history was the coming of the interstate highway system. This not only promised better transportation, but it also brought some short-lived construction jobs and served to remove large areas of slum housing from the local economy. Much of this housing was inadequate by modern standards, and the declining population caused high vacancy rates. The stretch of highway from Providence, Rhode Island, built to connect with Cape Cod, cut a swath right through the center of Fall River, taking even the City Hall. This symbolic threat to municipal identity may have come none too soon, as the building was in chronic disrepair. Only a few years earlier, pieces of the gold eagle fell from its peak, nearly killing a pedestrian and causing the whole area to be roped off until the bird could be made secure.

Today, Fall River is the poorest city in Massachusetts. Its median family income in 1969 was about 75 percent of the state's average, and its median level of education—8.8 years— ranked with poor counties of the rural South. Less than 5 percent of Fall River's population had a college education, and less than 2 percent were in the $25,000 income group.

Summary

Although sections of the United States seem to fit the model of a postindustrial society, it would be a mistake to view these parts as representing the whole. In the aggregate, the United States leads the world in sheer levels of wealth. Yet it also scores below numerous countries on measurements for equality of income, health care, housing, and literacy. Within the United States are several contrasts with postindustrial affluence; among them are the coal counties of Appalachia, sparsely settled communities along the southeastern coast of Alaska, the black belt of the rural South, and the long-depressed industrial cities of New England.

The next chapter looks beyond these economic and social indications of less-developed sectors in the United States. Its focus is on politics and public policy in the less-developed states, and how they look like counterparts to the poorest countries of Africa, Asia, and Latin America.

3

☆ ───────────────────────────────

LESS-DEVELOPED STATES
AND COUNTRIES

Every country has its poor people and its poor regions.
The concept of poverty, like that of development, is relative.
Virtually any economic condition can be described as "poor"
or "less developed" compared to some higher standard. If this
book did nothing more than point to some regions of the
United States that are poorer than others, it would be little
more than a semantic exercise focused on the concepts of
poverty and development. The argument is more complex
than a simple assertion about poverty in the United States. On
cross-national measures of economic equality and the quality
of life, the United States scores lower than it does on measures
of sheer wealth. Thus, on some important dimensions of
"economic development," this country scores somewhat below
the top of the heap. Moreover, internal contrasts in measures
of well-being are sharper here than in other seemingly developed countries, and here there are more people at the disadvantaged end of the contrasts.

This chapter pushes further into the complex argument about the status of the United States as a developing country. It shows that poor states are poor not only in economic traits, but that they also exhibit traits in politics, governmental structure, and public policy that resemble those found in the poor countries of Africa, Asia, and Latin America. These similarities suggest the depth of the drive for economic growth that occurs in the least-developed states as well as in the least-developed countries. They also suggest that the least-developed states and countries are pursuing similar strategies of economic growth.

There are obvious problems along the way to establishing credibility for a comparison of the least-developed American states and the least-developed countries of Africa, Asia, and Latin America. Our poor states benefit from the riches of the federal system, which offers both enormous financial aids for the state governments as well as a series of constitutional guarantees, statutes, and administrative regulations that provide some uniformity of governmental and political conditions from the most developed to the least developed of our states. This country has had a common market from its beginning, with a free flow of commerce, labor, and capital across state boundaries. On several measures, the poorest American state is more affluent than wealthier countries in Africa, Asia, and Latin America. Yet the least-developed countries and the least-developed states resemble one another in their relative lack of economic development even when they differ from one another in their absolute levels of development. Elites in each group aspire to economic growth, perhaps with different targets of aspiration. What is fascinating and commanding of explanation is the similarity among several elements of governmental form, politics, and public policy in the two groups of jurisdictions. They are truly *parallels*, i.e., similar but at different absolute levels of development.

Parallels between States and Countries

Several parallels appear to link the poor states of the United States with the poor countries of Africa, Asia, and Latin America. These include dependence on "foreign" sources of capital and policy leadership, the style of politicians, aspects of governmental structure, and public policy. In the United States, the prominent less-developed region is the South. Most of the following traits occur in most of the southern states, as well as in such other low-income states as Vermont, New Mexico, North Dakota, and Utah.[1]

Developing states and countries receive significant inputs of financial grants, soft loans, and technical assistance from other governments and from outside private capital. Chief among the governments that supply aid to the developing countries are the former colonial powers, with other assistance coming from a list of countries that features the United States, the Soviet Union, Canada, Sweden, and West Germany. In the United States, the federal government provides more in per capita aid to the developing states than do wealthier states. Per capita receipts of federal aid by state and local governments in the ten least-developed states were $160.51 during 1971–72, while they were $148.64 in other states. In the least-developed states, federal aid also bulked larger in relation to state and local funds raised from their own sources: 33.2 percent, compared to 22.1 percent in the other states. Low-income states also have relatively less private capital in local hands and depend more heavily on outside sources for investment. Per

1. The discussion that follows comes from Ira Sharkansky, "Structural Correlates of Least-Developed Economies: Parallels in Governmental Forms, Politics and Public Policies Among the Least-Developed Countries and the Least Developed (U.S.) States" (Paper delivered at the International Political Science Association Meetings, Montreal, August 1973).

capita assets of commercial banks in the ten least-developed states were $2,052 in 1971, while they were $3,858 in the other states.[2]

Citizens of both the developing states and developing countries feel they pay a price in the control of their economic resources by outsiders. Just as Chileans and Cubans have rallied against Yankee control of copper and sugar, so West Virginians, Kentuckians, and Georgians have declaimed Yankee control over their coal fields or railroads. A difference, of course, lies in the options open to the governments in the less-developed economies. A developing country may expropriate the resources of foreigners, but at the risk of substantial changes in international relations. Officials of the developing states in the United States have some leverage over "foreign" industry through the regulatory powers of the national government and the weight of their own representatives in the national legislature. Not all responses to outside control are peaceful or political. When a poor Georgia farmer burns his barn to collect the insurance, the label for the arson is "selling the farm to the Yankees." This reflects the local belief that northern insurance companies are in control and are more appropriate targets than a local company.

Developing states and countries rely on more advanced jurisdictions to supply models for government structures, procedures, and policies, which the less-well-off then adapt to their own circumstances. Developing countries began their independence with a heavy residue of governmental forms and procedures from their former colonial masters and continue looking to that source in adopting legislative and executive

2. The ten states ranking lowest on a widely used single indicator of economic development (per capita personal income) as of 1969 are Alabama, Arkansas, Kentucky, Louisiana, Mississippi, New Mexico, North Carolina, South Carolina, Tennessee, and West Virginia.

arrangements, civil-service codes, currency systems, and modes of providing services. In the United States, Professor Jack Walker has shown that lower-income states usually follow upper-income states in the adoption of new programs.[3]

Developing states and countries also resemble one another in certain efforts to induce economic growth. Both pursue industrialization with similar kinds of tax reductions for new industries or publicly constructed industrial plants, and both have problems with the marginal industries that are attracted by such schemes: firms that teeter on the brink of bankruptcy, require extensive nursing by officials charged with economic development, offer little in the way of transferable skills to their employees, or fail to pay back the government's investment in the form of substantial taxes or wages added to the economy. In the low-income states of the United States, the problem industries are small operations that employ low-skilled and low-paid workers, sometimes moving from one jurisdiction to another in order to take advantage of limited-term tax advantages or subsidized facilities. In developing countries, some problems come from marginal efforts at import substitution, resulting in higher-priced but poorer-quality goods than those available from importers. Other problems come from the showpiece heavy industries that strain a country's capacity to make available the skilled manpower needed to operate or manage the firm, to provide the markets needed to absorb its output, or to make the profits needed to repay foreign creditors.

The writings of state officials reveal a greater concern for economic growth in certain states, and a greater concern for conservation elsewhere. *State Government* is a journal published by the Council of State Governments that circulates

3. Jack L. Walker, "Innovation in State Politics," in *Politics in the American States: A Comparative Analysis,* ed. Herbert Jacob and Kenneth N. Vines (Boston: Little, Brown, 1971).

widely among individuals in policy-making positions of state administrative departments, governors' offices, and legislatures. The Spring 1973 issue featured articles about land-use policy which reveal clear differences between the approaches taken by Louisiana and Florida on the one hand, and Oregon on the other. Policies of Louisiana and Florida resemble those of poor countries, while Oregon fits the image of a postindustrial society.

One article drew a contrast between Louisiana and other states that rejected superport proposals because of environmental problems. In describing the situation, the director of Louisiana's Superport Authority used some classic stereotypes about the tired East:

> Overpopulated and suffering from advanced stages of urban decay, the East Coast wanted no part of anything that would lead to more industry, especially if it didn't understand the need.
>
> Of course, the situation on the Gulf Coast is quite different. . . . It is imperative that we attract new labor-intense industry and broaden our tax base. . . . Louisiana has learned well the lessons of the East Coast experience. Immediately after his election and before he took office, Louisiana Governor Edwin Edwards summoned top business, civic, environmental and shipping leaders to a conference to launch Louisiana's campaign for the now coveted facility. . . . If Louisiana is successful in obtaining a superport, it will probably be the most momentous event in the State since the discovery of oil, generating major new industry and thousands of new jobs.[4]

4. P. J. Mills, "A Supercatch for the Pelican State?" *State Government: The Journal of State Affairs* 46 (Summer 1973): 144–47.

Florida has built a large population with a policy of
boosting its climate, real estate, and agriculture. In 1950,
Florida ranked thirty-fifth in per capita income among the
states, and had moved up to twenty-ninth place by 1972. It lags
behind no other state in its record of persistently high growth
in population, and in its capacity to remake existing land and
water formations in the interest of growth. More recently,
some sectors of the state's population have caught the religion
of conservation. The city of Boca Raton received national
publicity for an ordinance limiting the number of housing
units, and thus its population. But Boca Raton is not typical of
Florida. It is a postindustrial enclave north of Miami. It
recorded some 31,000 residents in 1970, with 97.3 percent of
them white. Boca Raton's median family income is 46 percent
above the state average, and its single-family homes average
more than twice the statewide value. More typical of Florida's
posture toward growth and conservation is the 1972 Environmental Land and Water Management Act. Ostensibly, this was
an effort to provide state standards for development. However,
"in an effort to ensure that the Act could not be used to strangle
development," the legislature limited the amount of land
under state supervision to 5 percent of the total. Furthermore,
implementation rests heavily on the active participation of
local governments. An important role for "local effort" may
scuttle any pretense of "statewide" standards.[5] The Speaker of
the Florida House wrote:

> We have ... learned the phrase "growth policy" has
> several connotations to various people. Of course, to
> those whose interests are intimately connected with a

5. Richard G. Rubino, "An Evaluation: Florida's Land Use Law," *State
Government: The Journal of State Affairs* 46 (Summer 1973): 172–79.

growing Florida, there was an immediate suspicion that the growth policy was intended to be an anti-growth policy. In the early stages, however, a consensus was reached that Florida cannot arbitrarily halt its growth, both as a matter of practical economics and as a matter of legal and constitutional principle.[6]

Oregon is at the other extreme from Florida and Louisiana on growth policy. Former Governor McCall indentified himself with the slogan "Come Visit but Don't Stay." He gave active support to a state-required deposit on all beverage containers. He also advocated state incentives to urge new industry *away* from the Willamette Valley, and spoke publicly about withdrawing state support from tourist promotion. He does not want so many tourists that they overrun and destroy the beauty they came to enjoy. He has yet to advocate the slogan "Don't Visit," but he did urge a 40 percent reduction in the state's budget for tourist advertising and suggested using the remaining funds to direct tourists to less-well-visited parts of the state. McCall is proud of his reputation—and that of Oregon—for balancing the drive for growth with the conservation of existing amenities. In his contribution to *State Government's* symposium on land-use policy, he described several steps that his state has taken to refuse private industry proposals for development, or to require the sharp modification of other proposals.[7]

In both the least-developed countries and the least-developed states there is a greater role for cultural traditions in the political process. Political campaigns are less concerned

6. T. Terrell Sessums, "Legislating a Growth Policy," *State Government: The Journal of State Affairs* 47 (Spring 1974): 86.

7. Tom McCall, "Oregon: Come Visit but Don't Stay," *State Government: The Journal of State Affairs* 46 (Summer 1973): 167–71.

with the hard details of policy alternatives than with the efforts of candidates to identify themselves with folk symbols. In Kenya, for example, President Jomo Kenyatta features traditional dancing at many of his public appearances and often joins the dancers of different tribes to sway and kick through several routines. Likewise, an aspiring politician in the American South will mix with the folk and provide traditional food and music to attract them to his rallies. The importance of traditional symbols lies not so much in the food or festivities of political rallies, as in their use in cementing alliances and shaping the predisposition of policy makers. Developing countries and states provide examples where traditional loyalties slow the political modernization that is feasible. When the traditional symbols are racial or tribal in nature and serve to distinguish a ruling elite from the masses, traditionalism is likely to skew the distribution of policy benefits away from the left-out sectors of the population.

In his widely cited study of the American states, Daniel J. Elazar describes a *Traditional* culture that pervades most of the poor states, while Moralist and Individualist cultures prevail elsewhere. The Traditional culture, in Elazar's terms, eschews those activities of government that threaten the position of established elites. Thus it fits closely with the structural traits of governmental centralization and political concentration that also appear in the poor states.[8]

Two closely related and policy-relevant traits of politics also appear in least-developed jurisdictions here and abroad: governmental "centralization" and political "concentration." The centralization of government refers to the dominant role taken

8. Daniel J. Elazar, *American Federalism: A View from the States* (New York: Thomas Y. Crowell, 1972); and Robert E. Ward, "Political Modernization and Political Culture in Japan," in *Political Modernization: A Reader in Comparative Political Change*, ed. Claude E. Welch, Jr. (Belmont, Calif.: Duxbury, 1971), pp. 100–117.

by the central, as opposed to local governments. It shows in the center's collection of revenue, its distribution of financial aid to local units, its establishment of program standards to be followed by local governments, and its direct provision of services throughout the jurisdiction by means of central government officers. For the less-developed American states, the central government is the state government. Centralization appears most clearly in the ratios of state to local activities in revenue collection and spending. Over the 1958–72 period, the ten state governments with the least-developed economies provided 69.1 percent of their state plus local government revenues, while the ten state governments with the most-developed economies provided only 54.7 percent of their state plus local government revenues.[9]

For the least-developed countries, the best information about the relative positions of central and local governments comes from a doctoral dissertation written at the University of Southern California. Paulo Reis Vieira developed an index of decentralization for forty-five countries based upon the ratio of local government revenues and expenditures to total government revenue and expenditure for the period 1953–63. By comparing his country rankings with per capita gross domestic products, we find the expected association between economic development and decentralization. As in the case of the American states, governmental centralization is a trait of less-developed economies. The countries showing the greatest centralization on Vieira's index have an average gross domestic product per capita of $801, while the countries showing the

9. Centralization is measured as the percentage of combined state and local government tax revenues collected by the state or the percentage of combined state and local government expenditures made by the state (i.e., the central) government. For the data used in this section, the ten most-developed and the ten least-developed states are selected for their rankings on income per capita in the years 1958, 1960, 1962, 1964, 1966, 1968, 1970, 1972.

greatest *decentralization* have an average gross domestic product per capita of $2,647.[10]

Centralization in less-developed states and countries serves to maximize the central control of limited resources. In the United States, for example, when a state as a whole is poor, the local governments are especially poor. Rural counties and small towns cannot support state-mandated minimum levels of service on the basis of taxable resources that lie within their boundaries. It is the state government that has access to resources in *rich* as well as *poor* regions, and can use its taxes to acquire the sums necessary for programs throughout the state. The dynamics of politics work to extend state financial aids even to the rich communities. In order to pass the legislation needed to aid the low-income localities, there must be some aid for every locality. The result is a generally low level of local taxation throughout the least-developed states, with the state governments assuming financial responsibility for programs that are funded by local governments in the more-developed states.[11]

The field of elementary and secondary education provides some insight into the centralization of government in low-income American states. In much popular thinking, this area of policy belongs close to the grass roots. Local control of public schools has figured prominently in American history, extending back to their establishment in colonial New England

10. See Paulo Reis Vieira, "Toward a Theory of Decentralization: A Comparative View of Forty-Five Countries" (Ph.D. dissertation, University of Southern California, Los Angeles, 1967), cited in Frank P. Sherwood, "Devolution as a Problem of Organization Strategy," in *Comparative Urban Research: The Administration and Politics of Cities,* ed. Robert T. Daland (Beverly Hills: Sage, 1969), pp. 60–87; see also Francine F. Rabinovitz, "Urban Development and Political Development in Latin America," in ibid., pp. 88–123.

11. See Ira Sharkansky, *The Maligned States: Policy Accomplishments, Problems, and Opportunities* (New York: McGraw-Hill, 1972), pp. 59–62.

and forward to the demands for local control of schools during the last two decades. On some issues—like who determines the racial mixture—local schools are not autonomous. Over the years, state governments have developed extensive standards with respect to minimum qualifications for teachers, the length of the school year, and the consolidation of small rural districts. Each state provides sizable funds for local school aid, with some of the money used to induce local compliance with state guidelines. Local control of schools remains important, however. Over the country as a whole, some 51 percent of elementary and secondary school budgets come from local sources; and local authorities exercise important discretion with respect to the selection of teachers, salaries, curriculum, textbooks, and extracurricular activities. As the latest clashes over school busing indicate, expressions in behalf of local autonomy are still heard on the streets and in official circles, including the Nixon and Ford White Houses.

We can see in the realm of school finance, however, a peculiarity of the less-developed states. In the ten states having the lowest incomes per capita, the percentage of school funds coming from local sources was only 28.0 during 1972-73, with 55.4 percent coming from the state government and 16.7 percent from Washington. For the other states, the record shows 57.0 percent from local sources, 37.4 percent from the states, and only 5.5 percent from the national government. Three of the low-income states receive less than 25 percent of their school funds from local sources: Alabama, Mississippi, and New Mexico. In some low-income states, annual decisions in the state government deal with issues that are handled locally elsewhere: the legislature debates the salaries of schoolteachers, and the state board of education offers a short list of textbooks for each course, from which local officials make the final selection.

We must avoid exaggerating the power of the central government in the least-developed states and countries, even while we accept the finding of governmental centralization. There is much commentary about the power of tribal or regional elites in Africa and parts of Asia, but this is usually couched in terms of impediments to the effectiveness of central government institutions. There is little indication that regional or local *structures of government* exercise any major roles in the formulation of policies. The distinction is important; central governments in many developing countries are weakened by problems of linguistic or ethnic integration, communication, control, and legitimacy that keep them from asserting their formal powers into the regions, but they are not made weak by countervailing governments in the regions. What government exists tends to be in the center. No federal systems in the developing countries function as federalism does in the United States. Public administration is national in the nature of its career service; virtually all commentaries and compilations of public finance emphasize the revenues collected by the central government; central government ministries control the design and implementation of public services ranging from higher education to rural development.[12]

We must also avoid exaggerating the power of the central (i.e., state) governments in the least developed of the American states. These states show some traits (e.g., extralegal regional powerholders and cultural norms) found in the least-developed countries that work against state government controls. As in the least-developed countries, however, what government exists tends to be in the center. State governments in lower-income states tend to exercise significant powers in setting tax rates and making policies for schools, highways, and

12. See, for example, Robert B. Bangs, *Financing Economic Development: Fiscal Policy for Emerging Countries* (Chicago: University of Chicago Press, 1968).

welfare that are within the control of local governments in more affluent jurisdictions.

Concentration pertains to the aggregation of political options in relatively few hands, and reflects citizens' opportunities to influence policies. It differs from *centralization*, which signifies the aggregation of powers to officials in the capital city. Yet concentration and centralization complement one another: both permit a narrow base of effective participation, with many citizens and officials left out of real decision making.

A hallmark of concentration is limited competition between political parties. The dominance of single parties lessens the opportunities for citizens to make decisions on the basis of alternatives to present officeholders or public policies. In some developing countries, the major party has a monopoly written into the national laws and enforced by the official police or party thugs.[13]

In many low-income American states, the lack of party competition coincides with a low incidence of voter turnout. Lack of participation presumably reflects the lack of importance and interest that attaches to noncompetitive election. In the ten states with the least-developed economies, the majority party won an average 62.9 percent of the vote in gubernatorial elections over the 1958–72 period, and turnout rates averaged 34.6 percent of the age-eligible population; comparable figures for the ten states with the most-developed economies showed

13. See, for example, William J. Foltz, "Building the Newest Nations: Short-Run Strategies and Long-Run Problems," and James S. Coleman and Carl Rosberg, Jr., "African One-Party States and Modernization," both in Claude E. Welch, Jr., *Political Modernization: A Reader in Comparative Political Change* (Belmont, Calif.: Duxbury, 1971), pp. 293–304, 330–54; and Aristide R. Zolberg, *Creating Political Order: The Party-States of West Africa* (Chicago: University of Chicago Press, 1966).

closer divisions in the electorate (54.1 percent of the gubernatorial vote won by the majority party) and more turnout (57.7 percent).[14]

Some developing countries score high on voter turnout because of mandatory participation and the emphasis placed on voting by mass-mobilization parties. Widespread participation in politics occurs in an authoritarian context where the citizens lack the opportunity to lend their support to real alternatives in ways that make a difference for issues of public policy. For these reasons, we cannot compare the least-developed states and the least-developed countries on the same indicator of political participation.

Many political scientists who specialize in the study of American states have been preoccupied with the linkages between economic resources, party competition, and the character of state policy. It is significant for the argument of this book that a classic formulation of these connections appeared in a book about the South, V. O. Key's *Southern Politics*. Professor Key argued that the lack of competition between political parties was important in explaining the skimpy character of social-welfare programs in the region. Without competitive parties seeking voter support, a political mechanism to bid up the level of public services was missing. Key's book appeared in 1949, and argued its point by means of careful description and simple statistics. With the arrival of computers and social scientists trained in their use during the 1960s and 1970s, there came a series of books and articles in professional journals seeking to test Key's propositions. The basic questions at issue were: *Does competition between state political parties affect the character of state policies?* and *Is the level of economic development in a state the primary influence on*

14. Turnouts are measured in contests for the U.S. House of Representatives; data come from *Statistical Abstracts of the United States, 1960–74*.

both competition and on policy, with competition stronger in the wealthy states than in the poorer states? A complex and occasionally heated debate continues among the scholars, with the findings differing according to how they measure various items for economic development, competition, and policy, and what computational techniques they use to test statistical relationships. There is general agreement, however, that the elements of economics, competition, and policy are linked together in some way, and that the low-income states generally have less competition for state offices.[15]

Strong executive leadership frequently accompanies the traits of centralization and concentration. Huey Long is the archetype of a strong executive in the context of a less-developed American state, with George Wallace, Gene Talmadge, and Orval Faubus providing other examples. Virtually all the developing countries offer their own parallels. Among the more striking cases are those nationalist leaders who led their countries out of the colonial experience: Kwame Nkrumah in Ghana, Jomo Kenyatta in Kenya, Julius Nyerere in Tanzania, Hastings Banda in Malawi, and Sukarno in Indonesia. In almost all of the least-developed countries, it is the bureaucracy—and often the military sector of the bureaucracy—that joins the chief executive in commanding the greatest leverage in public policy. The bureaucracy attracts members of the best families and the brightest graduates of the national universities; it commands a virtual monopoly over

15. For samples of this research, see Herbert Jacob and Kenneth N. Vines, eds., *Politics in the American States: A Comparative Analysis* (2nd ed.; Boston: Little, Brown, 1971). The research for this book actually began in this genre. The research indicates that traits described for the low-income states in this chapter are not simply the mirror images of traits appearing for the upper-income states. In other words, there appears to be a clustering of traits for lower-income states—those that make them appear in many respects like the poor countries—without these traits being distributed in a linear fashion according to income among all the states.

technical expertise; and its police and military may use their powers to control other branches of government.[16]

A trait of strong leaders in both poor states and poor countries is their posturing as defenders of traditional local values against powerful and hostile outsiders. In poor countries this takes the form of the national leader who fought for independence, and who continues to defend against the forces of colonialism or neo-colonialism. The American analog is the southern politician—e.g., George Wallace—who stands in the schoolhouse door against the court orders of federal marshals and campaigns against "the briefcase-toting bureaucrats" from Washington.

Much of the recent writing about chief executives points to the impediments in the way of the government head who wishes to dominate state (or national) policy. The principal barriers are said to be competitive politics, strong legislatures, and a professional bureaucracy—i.e., the kinds of features that appear in the national government of the United States and in many of its states with large populations, diverse economies, and two competitive political parties. Under these conditions, the chief executive is more likely to be a leader who persuades, cajoles, and bargains with strong protagonists than a truly dominant figure who issues instructions and leaves a distinctive, personal mark on government policy.[17] The heroic figures in government who have legislators and bureaucrats eating out of their hands are thought to occur more typically in new countries amid political turmoil or in the relatively simple

16. See, for example, Fred W. Riggs, *Administration in Developing Countries: The Theory of Prismatic Society* (Boston: Houghton Mifflin, 1964).

17. See Richard Neustadt, *Presidential Power: The Politics of Leadership* (New York: Wiley, 1960); and John F. Manley, *The Politics of Finance: The House Committee on Ways and Means* (Boston: Little, Brown, 1970). A more recent body of literature deals with the presidential excesses of the Watergate period. It is significant for the Neustadt view, however, that the Nixon Presidency tumbled with the cooperation of some of the President's own appointees.

American settings of rural states with relatively small populations and one dominant political party.

Vice-President Nelson A. Rockefeller is a significant exception to the principles that associate strong executives with simple states. He served as governor of New York from 1959 to his resignation in 1973. That tenure alone makes him outstanding in a state at or very near the top in its population size, social and economic diversity, and competitive two-party politics. Moreover, his record as a policy maker during that period was also outstanding: he was closely identified with a multibillion-dollar building program at the government center in Albany, and with an even more costly expansion of public higher education. What is the explanation for his duration and his success as a policy maker? Several aspects of his situation fit that great cliché of writers and teachers: the exception that proves the rule. In this case, the rule argues against strong executives in large, complex, competitive, and politically stable states or countries. Why the exception? Partly because New York's politics are not as competitive for state officeholders as they seem from an examination of all the registered Democrats in the electorate. During Rockefeller's period as governor, the state Democratic party was beset with such great factional strife that only a deus ex machina like Robert F. Kennedy could win a major state race as a Democrat. Also, the Republicans enjoyed majorities in both houses of New York's legislature during most of Rockefeller's tenure.

To explain Rockefeller's success as a policy maker, we may also call upon some information that became available during the hearings into his nomination as vice-president. In his period as governor he gave upward of $850,000 in gifts to key people who served as policy makers or advisers. There has been no sign that these funds were tendered as quid pro quo for actions wanted by the governor to enact his proposals. The sums nevertheless reflect Rockefeller's great wealth, and his generosity to individuals who serve well. He also made no secret of the fact that he wanted to be President during much of his gubernatorial administration. He was a wealthy and potentially rising star who represented future rewards of high political association if not outright financial benefits. Such assets in the usual policy-making process of persuasion, cajoling, and bargaining were available to few of Rockefeller's contemporaries in the American states.

Regressive tax and spending policies also link the developing states and countries. A regressive tax or expenditure is one that takes disproportionately from the lower-income population or provides its benefits disproportionately to upper-income classes. In developing states and countries, the regressive tax has the advantage of taking revenue from the large number of poor residents who may possess—in the aggregate—more of the money and account for most of the taxable transactions. A regressive tax also does not burden the wealthy, and thus leaves them free to invest in commerce or industry that may add to economic growth. In the developing countries, the typical regressive taxes are excise taxes on fuel, cloth, processed food, beer, or manufactured goods; and customs duty on goods that permeate the society (e.g., imported radios and printed cloth, or the imported components assembled by local industries). In some countries, regressive levies do not exist as separate commodity taxes but are included within the price of goods manufactured or distributed by government corporations. Such corporations are expected to make a profit on their transactions, with the surplus going to the government treasury as a tax on the corporation, or used to pay for the services or the subsidies provided to certain citizens directly by the corporation.

In the United States, the archetype of the regressive tax is the levy on retail sales. State individual and corporate income taxes, in contrast, are progressive.[18] Over the 1958–72 period, the ten states with the least-developed economies drew only 17.6 percent of their revenues from income taxes and 30.5 percent from sales taxes; in contrast, the ten states with the most-developed economies took 24.3 percent of their revenues from income taxes and only 21.3 percent from sales taxes.

The tendency to avoid progressive taxes has a further parallel in the tendency to give little support to those programs that have a progressive impact on the distribution of resources. Elementary and secondary education, welfare and public health programs go disproportionately to citizens in the lower-income ranges;[19] in the United States, these programs tend to receive smaller per capita allocations in the low-income states. Over the 1958–72 period, education and welfare spending averaged $177.34 per capita in the ten low-income states, and $231.39 per capita in the ten high-income states. Highway construction and the development of natural resources, in contrast, represent investments in economic infrastructure and promise "growth"; one study finds them receiving greater per capita allocations in states with less-developed industrial sectors.[20] In 1970 and 1972, the low-income states averaged $86.50 per capita for highway spending, while the upper-income states averaged only $84.10 per capita. Similar allocations appear in the development plans of many lower-income countries and serve to complement their avoidance of progressive taxes. On the expenditure side, these plans feature transportation, electric power, and communications, which promise economic growth and give their most direct benefits to middle- and upper-income persons with capital to invest or the training needed for the new job opportunities.

18. See *Allocating Tax Burdens and Government Benefits by Income Class* (New York: Tax Foundation, 1967).
19. Ibid.
20. Ira Sharkansky and Richard I. Hofferbert, "Dimensions of State Policy," in Jacob and Vines, *Politics in the American States.*

Most of the social-welfare programs offered by the low-income states receive some financial contributions from the national government. This blurs the state's effort by not allowing us to see how much the poor states would do for their needy citizens if it were not for the national government's money and program requirements. Occasionally, we can see what the states do on their own. One welfare program not aided by federal funds or covered by federal requirements is variously labeled *general relief, general assistance,* or *poor relief.* State or local governments can make this program available from their own funds, according to criteria they establish. For the most part, "general assistance" provides for needs left unmet by federally aided programs for the aged, blind, disabled, or families with dependent children.

In many localities of the poor states, there is no general assistance at all! A 1966 report by the United States Department of Health, Education, and Welfare showed general assistance activities, by county, for each of forty-one states that complied fully with the Department's questionnaire. (It is in the nature of general assistance that reporting requirements may be so casual as to hinder analysis.) Nine of the ten lowest-income states reported general assistance activities by county, and there were *no* general assistance expenditures in some 32 percent of their counties. Other states showed no general assistance in only 12 percent of their counties. Several of the poorest states had no general assistance in a majority of their counties: 52 percent of the counties in Mississippi, 61 percent in Alabama, and 65 percent in Kentucky listed no expenditures. Even when counties reported some activity, the amounts could be pitifully small. Alabama's average expenditure per case for the month reported was $12.50; Claiborne and Walthall counties in Mississippi spent about $5.00 per case; Franklin and Jessamine counties in Kentucky made average grants of $4.35 and $4.75 per case. In these and numerous other counties in the poor states, county officials provided nothing more than an occasional meal, or sometimes a one-way bus ticket or a tank of gasoline so an indigent could leave the county. And in many other counties there was no public aid forthcoming for the very poor who did not qualify for the federally aided programs.

More recent figures, available for statewide average payments under general assistance, show that low-income states remain considerably below the others. In June 1973 average grants were $29.05 per recipient in the ten poorest states, and $74.56 in the others. This differential between the less-developed states and the others is greater than in welfare programs where federal money and standards narrowed the gaps. In the field of old-age assistance, for example, the average grant for the ten poorest states was $67.78, and that for in the remaining states was $83.04. Thus, the differential for the federally aided and controlled program was a factor of 1.23 times between the ten poorest states and the rest, while the differential for general assistance was a factor of 2.57 times.

The Policy Relevance of Parallels

Elements of governmental centralization, political concentration, traditionalism in politics, and such policies as industrial promotion and tax and spending regressivity fit together in a syndrome that both reflects conditions of relative deprivation and may affect the processes of further economic development. Regressive taxes allow the central government to amass significant wealth in a poor state or country, which then becomes available for public investment, even while affluent citizens are taxed only lightly and may invest their wealth in the development of the private sector. Centralization and concentration both serve to limit the claimants on public resources. Centralization provides only a minimum opportunity for regional and local groups to bolster their demands on public resources with the aid of any formal instruments built into the policy-making process. Political concentration lessens the power of citizens in regional or class groupings who would claim resources for their own welfare purposes. The ballyhoo of traditional symbols in political campaigns may distract unsophisticated voters from regressive policies which burden the poor and benefit the rich.

According to one view, prospects for economic development benefit from centralization, concentration, traditionalism, and regressive policies. Yet this view is problematical and relies on one important assumption: the elite that benefits will use its economic and political leverage for the public good rather than private gain. Programs of industrialization, transportation, communication, and improved agricultural techniques can result from a public-minded elite investing rationally to stimulate economic development, even while it economizes by holding down expenditures for social welfare. On the other hand, some elites use their leverage to reinforce their own position, keep taxes low for their own social class, control the government for personal profit, and either bank the proceeds elsewhere or consume them in opulence at home. The developing states and countries provide examples both of asceticism and excess on the part of their elites.

Some Exceptions and the Issue of Regional Peculiarity

Not all jurisdictions in the "least developed" categories fit each component of the centralization-concentration-regressivity syndrome. Among the developing countries, India presents an exceptional record of political competition; it also joins

Nigeria in having a federal structure of government. But in neither case do the state or regional governments exhibit the degree of financial or programmatic independence of the central government shown by American states. The central government in India has used its powers to alter state boundaries unilaterally, and to remove sitting governors from office. India and a number of other developing countries also show the rudiments of a progressive income tax. In most cases, however, these taxes account for a small percentage of government revenue; their potential is made weak by the combination of a low incidence of upper-income citizens who qualify for the tax and problems of taxpayer ignorance and avoidance, plus few of the administrative resources needed for audit and collection.[21] Several notable exceptions among the American states also deserve attention: West Virginia for its unusually high rates of political competition and participation,[22] and Louisiana for its progressive taxes on incomes and the extraction of natural resources.[23]

In much of the literature on the American states, it is common to ask if the findings are simply a function of southern peculiarities. This question is especially relevant to the current issue, insofar as the southern states are the least developed economically yet have traits of social and political conservatism that may produce elements of traditionalism, centralization, concentration, and regressivity independent of the southern economy.[24] To test this possibility, table 3.1 identifies the eight nonsouthern states with the least-developed economies and compares their scores on measures of centralization, concentration, and regressivity to those of the ten states with

21. See Bangs, *Financing Economic Development.*
22. Sharkansky and Hofferbert, "Dimensions of State Policy."
23. For a description of the era that produced these distinctive traits in Louisiana's policies, see T. Harry Williams, *Huey Long* (Boston: Little, Brown, 1969).
24. Ira Sharkansky, *Regionalism in American Politics* (Indianapolis: Bobbs-Merrill, 1969).

the best-developed economies. It is true that the least-developed nonsouthern states generally show the traits of centralization, concentration, and regressivity less consistently than their southern counterparts. Yet New Mexico and Vermont differ from the wealthiest states, as expected, by showing higher scores on centralization and concentration, and lower scores on the use of progressive income taxes; and North Dakota and Utah fit the expectations on two of the three measures. Further, these nonsouthern states are better developed economically than most of the southern states discussed earlier in this chapter and so should fit the centralization-concentration-regressivity syndrome less closely. Thus there is some basis for concluding that more than "southernness" leads low-income states to show the traits identified as parallels with the poor countries.

Table 3.1. **Scores of the Least-Developed Nonsouthern States on Measures of Centralization, Concentration, and Regressivity**

	State Percentage of State Tax Revenue	*Majority Party Percentage of State Legislature*	*Percentage of Revenue in Income Taxes*
Idaho	62.9	57.1	21.8
Maine	54.9	53.6	7.9
Montana	46.6	53.5	16.0
New Mexico	74.9	67.9	7.3
North Dakota	52.4	65.3	7.5
South Dakota	42.4	62.7	0.2
Utah	63.3	54.6	13.6
Vermont	64.5	65.6	18.0
Mean score for ten states with most-developed economies*	54.8	61.6	20.6

*As ranked on income per capita.

Source: State Government Finances, 1969–71 (Washington, D.C.: U.S. Government Printing Office, 1970–72).

Mississippi as a Developing State

Mississippi is an excellent example of a low-income American state that exhibits many traits of a developing country. The 1970 Census data score it at or near the bottom of state rankings on measures of personal income; infant mortality; quality of housing; and availability of health care, schools, and library facilities. H. L. Mencken once dubbed it "The Worst State." On each item featured in the centralization-concentration-regressivity syndrome, Mississippi scores as expected: 74.0 percent of state and local taxes are collected by the state government; the Democratic party controlled 97.7 percent of the seats in the state legislature in 1970; only 24.9 percent of the voting-age population cast ballots in the elections of 1970; and the state government collects only 7.0 percent of its revenue in the form of individual or corporate income taxes.

Mississippi is not simply a typical state on the dimensions of the centralization-concentration-regressivity syndrome; it is archetypal. It is a rural state, with its industrial sector new and for the most part small-scale. It is known throughout the world as the place where American norms of democracy and personal liberty encounter their most narrow limits. For many years it had the forms of democracy but required the enactment of federal statutes and the actions of federal courts and law-enforcement agencies to make those forms real. In these traits Mississippi resembled countless poor countries with constitutions copied from the United States, Great Britain, or France, but with authoritarian practices.[25] Politics is tough in Mississippi. Citizens who oppose the status quo must anticipate problems with respect to fair treatment of their cam-

25. See Riggs, *Administration in Developing Countries,* for his discussion of "formalism."

paigns in the mass media, economic sanctions against voters who support their movement, and physical intimidations that may go unchecked by law-enforcement agencies.

Mississippi stands out for the regressivity of its tax policies. It invented the retail sales tax in 1933 as a mechanism that would collect sizable revenues in a low-income jurisdiction made even poorer by a major depression. Persons bought mill tokens and surrendered them to merchants when making even the tiniest purchase. Within eight years, twenty-one states copied Mississippi's tax innovation, and the tax on retail sales was on its way to becoming the largest single source of revenue for American state governments. Mississippi taxes individual incomes but does this in a way to minimize any potential for progressive rates. The personal income tax includes only two brackets: a rate of 3 percent on incomes to $5,000 and 4 percent on higher incomes. Above $5,000, progressivity stops. Median family income in Mississippi was $6,068 as early as 1969, meaning that the majority of residents are in the highest-income bracket for state tax purposes. As recently as 1971, the state allowed a personal deduction for a spouse, but none for children. In Mississippi this meant that a large number of low-income, husbandless females with children found little protection in the rate structure or exemptions.

With all its features of political concentration and regressive taxes, Mississippi does not present a simple case of an economic and political elite looking after its own interests. Despite its impoverished economy, the state government raises and spends a great deal of money. On a measure of "tax effort," Mississippi ranked thirteenth in the country during 1970–71 on revenues per $1,000 of personal income raised by state and local governments, exclusive of federal aid. Mississippi spends heavily on several programs that claim to promote economic development: higher education, highways, and health-hospitals. It structures its tax system to encourage the in-migration of upper-income residents who might invest in the state, and it has an active program to promote investments in industry and agriculture. Mississippi may deserve the scorn of observers in poor countries, who attack it as a symbol of racism in the United States. Yet it also deserves their attention as the American state whose economics and politics look most like their own, and whose policies combine features of regressivity and investment for growth.

Differences between Developing States and Developing Countries

This concern for similarities and parallels between the developing states of the United States and developing countries should not blind us to important differences between them. These differences affect their opportunities for economic growth and their rates of growth, even though important similarities remain in governmental structures, political processes, and policy elements that also affect those growth prospects.

The most prominent difference between the least-developed American states and the least-developed countries is their level of present development. The ten least-developed states enjoy per capita income in the range of $3,100–$3,700. Even allowing for problems encountered when comparing different measurements, living standards, price of basic commodities, and the extent of nonmarket sectors in the developing countries, these figures signal great differences from the range of $85–$110 per capita gross national product that we find in the least-developed countries. Related to these differences are the generally uniform access in the United States to elementary and secondary education, at least rudimentary health care, and the nationally supported systems of public assistance and social insurance. Comparable programs appear only as rare luxuries in most regions of Asia, Africa, and Latin America. We should not forget the common-market features, with no customs or currency controls, of the American economy which has facilitated the movement of labor and capital to sites of opportunity. There are also massive differences in the amounts of outside financial aid coming to developing states and countries. In 1971–72, federal assistance to state and local governments averaged $160.51 per capita in the ten least-developed states; an estimate of foreign aid to the developing countries puts the figure at $1.00–$2.00 per capita annually for recent years.[26] Each of the least-developed American states has two senators and a number of congressmen who work to create national programs that foster economic development, and to assure favorable decisions in the federal bureaucracy about projects back home. None of the least-developed countries has such steady access to foreign aid. Even while some countries have benefited from favorable positions in international politics—e.g., South Korea, Taiwan, South Vietnam, and Israel—none has Mississippi's guarantee of steady entrée to the United States Treasury.

Partly because of this financial aid from the national government, economic differences between the least-developed and most-developed states have had a declining influence on their public policies during the course of the twentieth century. The federal government has made up for some of the economic differentials that exist "naturally" among the states, with the result that economic traits of the states now have about one-third the impact on state and local government policies that was observed for the beginning of the century.[27]

26. Bangs, *Financing Economic Development,* pp. 83–88.
27. See Alan K. Campbell and Seymour Sacks, *Metropolitan America: Fiscal Patterns and Governmental Systems* (New York: Free Press, 1967), p. 57.

In these signs of public affluence, we see the benefits to our developing sectors from their existence in a country that is both developing and developed. Because of barriers in their access to affluence, the governments of the least-developed countries face greater difficulties in their pursuit of economic growth. It is also the misfortune of the least-developed countries to arrive on the scene at a time when people seem less willing to ignore or accept their deprivations than in the eras when the countries of Western Europe and North America achieved their development.

Do these differences between the least-developed countries and the least-developed states outweigh the parallels? The answer depends partly on one's perspective. From the American context, the parallels should remind us of the depth of poor sectors in this country and the role of further development in their plans for the future. The discovery of political parallels in two groups of jurisdictions that differ so much in absolute terms calls attention to the relative lack of economic development in which the jurisdictions resemble one another. Moreover, the specific points of resemblance—traditionalism, centralization, concentration, and regressivity—suggest the similar strategies that are being used in the pursuit of economic development.

Parallels in Early America

This book focuses on contemporary comparisons between poor American states and poor countries. Still, it is helpful to cite additional parallels between these contexts and the early history of the American national government. The syndrome of governmental centralization, political concentration, and regressive tax policies was present in the United States of the eighteenth and nineteenth centuries, although it has been partly masked by elements treated more prominently by historians. With a bit of searching, we can find components of the syndrome and view them in the context of a new nation concerned with economic development.[28]

Governmental centralization is the element of the syndrome that is most difficult to spot in the early United States. The country was actually more *decentralized* than it is today. State legislatures elected United States senators; an elaborate method of electing the President depended on separate actions in each state government; and James Madison stated in *Federalist #46* that "beyond doubt ... the first and most natural attachment of the people will be to the governments of their respective states." Yet the Constitution that gave rise to this statement by Madison represented a major, and successful, effort at government centralization. To be sure, the change toward centralization did not proceed as far as some of the framers wanted. Hamilton in particular sought a stronger central government than was produced. Nevertheless, the country entered the constitutional era with a far stronger central government than existed under the Articles of Confederation. Lawmakers in Washington were no longer beholden to state governments for instructions and salaries; the national government could levy its own taxes and raise men for its armed services without waiting on the voluntary actions of the states; there was a vigorous President and only vague constitutional limits against his authority; and a Supreme Court was soon to give weight to the constitutional language that indicated the national government was supreme.

In the *Federalist Papers* we can find explicit links between a strengthened national government and the economic future of the country. In *Federalist #11,* Alexander Hamilton wrote:

28. Seymour Martin Lipset, *The First New Nation: The United States in Historical and Comparative Perspective* (Garden City, N.Y.: Anchor, 1967).

The importance of the Union, in a commercial light, is one of those points about which there is least room to entertain a difference of opinion. . . .

Under a vigorous national government, the natural strength and resources of the country, directed to a common interest, would baffle all the combinations of European jealousy to restrain our growth.

Political concentration and tax regressivity both appear in the early history of the United States. Political participation was at first limited to a small group. The Constitution recognized the status of slavery and the absence of popular elections for the President and Senate. Several of the states and many localities placed further restrictions on the suffrage, usually pertaining to religion and wealth. Sex existed as a barrier to suffrage until 1920, and eighteen-year-olds could not vote throughout the country until 1972.

The tax system of the United States resembled that of contemporary developing countries until the 1920s. Only then did a progressive tax on income begin in a continuing way to collect more revenue for the national government than did excise taxes and custom duties. The spending policies of the early national government lends further weight to its comparison with contemporary developing countries. Welfare payments did not become apparent until the 1930s. The first century of the national budget featured heavy public investments in infrastructure: roads, canals, railways, banking, the westward movement of the population, and the exploitation of agricultural resources. Education was the only concern of the early national government that might fit a classification of "welfare." Yet Washington's spending for education was meager until the 1950s; and as we see in the contemporary developing world, education is made attractive for a new country when viewed as "manpower development."

Summary

This chapter stops short of equating the least-developed American states with the least-developed countries, or of positing a new theory of economic growth. Yet it does show that the poorest states and the poorest countries have traits in common that are made important by likely relationships with their mutual pursuit of economic development. The syndrome of traditionalism in politics, government centralization, political concentration, and the regressivity of tax and spending policies may further economic growth—provided, perhaps, that elites use their advantages for public rather than private purposes, and provided also that the population does not so chafe at arrangements as to cause political or economic instability.

There are several implications of this shared syndrome. Political scientists who concentrate on developing countries should test more of their constructs with data from the American states. Students of the states should judge more of their own theories for political change and policy making with respect to the experiences of other countries. Policy makers in the developing countries should look to the least developed of the American states for patterns to emulate, rather than to wealthier states or to the national government of the United States. The states at the lower end of our spectrum approach the developing countries most closely in the scale of activities as well as in the nature of their economic and political problems. It is improbable that state officials of Mississippi or national officials in Africa, Asia, or Latin America will enjoy these comparisons. Yet each may learn from the others' experience, no matter how embarrassing the effort.

4

☆ ──────────────────────────────────

LESS-DEVELOPED
URBAN SECTORS

The cities present two sides of America. Their attractive side includes productive manufacturing, innovative service industries, striking architecture, and experimental programs on the frontiers of social policy. Their unattractive side features slum housing, grinding poverty, widespread crime and attendant social programs that seem unable to cope with people's needs, and occasional disorders that threaten the political fabric. Depending on which side receives attention, the cities of the United States may be described as advanced or underdeveloped on the world scale.

The presence of these two sides in American cities adds up to *dualism.* This is the presence of contrasting economic and social phenomena in close proximity. It is a trait found in cities throughout Africa, Asia, and Latin America. In the poor countries it appears as the *favelas* or shantytowns erected out of mud, grass, or packing crates within sight of high-rise steel-and-glass buildings. A common pattern in the United States finds rotting tenements, filth, vermin, and social pathologies within walking distance of attractive business buildings and affluent dwellings. Our cities present this country's sharpest contrasts in closest proximity between rich and poor. A view of the United States as a developing country must deal with the cities. There the argument finds some of its best evidence. If our social and economic problems anywhere threaten the body politic on the model of an unstable developing country, that threat comes in the cities.

This chapter considers both sides of the dualism in America's cities: the misery of poverty and the resources of affluence. It does not lose sight of the larger context in which cities exist. This country is in part developing, but it is also highly developed. On the strength of its resources, it has the wherewithal to address some problems of its less-developed sectors. In the recent history of American cities, we can see this process at work. Our largest cities are able to deal with at least some features of their lagging development.

The Crisis of Central Cities

Dualism in America's cities is widely commented upon, although it is seldom referred to as dualism per se. More often, it is described as the sharp divergence between middle-class standards and the actual conditions found in personal incomes, education, employment opportunities, housing, health, and crime.

The worst of this urban crisis is said to be in the central cities of the large metropolitan areas. Poor whites as well as poor blacks and other ethnic minorities live there, but it is the blacks and other minorities who present the most serious concentrations of poverty and who suffer numerous other social dislocations that seem based upon, and feed, their poverty. They endure the highest rate of unemployment and under-employment; they are segregated in low-quality schools; their crime and disease rate are highest; and they have meager opportunities for decent housing and public recreation.

Among the problems that reinforce the poverty of the central-city residents are:

1. Educational programs and teachers that are unresponsive to the social and linguistic problems of the urban poor and unable to provide the training necessary to maximize their economic potential
2. Unemployment concentrations among males eighteen to twenty-five years old with little education, which makes them highly visible and susceptible recruits for civil disorder
3. Dispersion of industrial and commercial jobs to the suburbs, beyond easy commuting range of the central-city labor pool
4. Failure of mass transit to meet the needs of low-income communities for cheap home-to-job transportation
5. Poor diets resulting in low stamina for school and job performance
6. High rates of infant mortality and mental retardation, traceable in part to inadequate prenatal care and infant diets
7. High rates of venereal disease and illegitimacy, with attendant problems of fatherless homes and delinquency passing through the generations
8. Substandard housing, plus social and economic barriers against the dispersion of low-income minority populations to better neighborhoods
9. High crime rates in poor neighborhoods, which reflect social dislocations and add to the burdens carried by neighborhood residents

The city dweller's response to these problems is heightened by a view of government as incapable of correcting them. Local governments are said to lack the ability to deal with such problems, and state and federal governments fail to provide the resources necessary. Some federal policies, by encouraging suburban sprawl, actually aggravate rather than alleviate urban problems.

It is an irony of the urban scene that the cities contain great concentrations of wealth but are unable to pay for their social needs. If, for purposes of analysis, we lump together the big cities and their suburbs and describe the wealth of metropolitan areas, we find:

—More than four-fifths of the nation's financial capital, as measured by the deposits in banks and savings and loan associations
—More than three-fourths of the industrial wealth, as measured by value added by manufacturing
—Three-fourths of the personal income

All these proportions of the nation's wealth are greater than the 69 percent of the nation's population that lives in metropolitan areas. Metropolitan residents also have more education than nonmetropolitan residents, and metropolitan communities are growing relative to others.[1]

The great problem of urban policy is that local governments cannot tap private wealth for public programs. Metropolitan areas are demographic but not governmental entities. We cannot lump the big cities and their suburbs for purposes of policy making. Many reformers have tried, but few have succeeded. Numerous governments compete for the private wealth in urban areas. The state and national govern-

1. This section relies on Robert L. Lineberry and Ira Sharkansky, *Urban Politics and Public Policy* (New York: Harper & Row, 1974), chap. 2.

ments soak up huge amounts through their income and sales taxes, and a surplus of suburbs and special districts divide the funds available from taxes on urban real estate. The central cities are caught between the migration of big taxpayers to the suburbs and the competition from state and federal tax systems. Local officials are susceptible to the argument that high taxes will keep away—or drive away—property owners who would otherwise make substantial contributions to the local economy. Also, the anachronistic formulas of some state and federal aids provide greater benefits to wealthy suburbs than to struggling central cities.

Poor Suburbs

In several of the larger metropolitan areas there are parallels to the central-city problems in independent suburbs. In contrast to the myth of affluence that prevails about surburban communities, their reality is more of a mixture. There are working-class, ethnic, and black suburbs; there are commercial and industrial suburbs; and there are those that fit the common stereotype. Some of the sharpest social and economic differences in the metropolitan areas appear in comparisons of upper-class white and working-class black or racially mixed suburbs. For the people at the lower end of these comparisons, the problems may be even greater than in the ghettos of central cities. The problems of poor suburbanites are made more difficult in a world of limited resources where demands must be highly visible in order to be met. Moreover, the independent suburb—unlike the black neighborhood of the central city—is responsible for local tax collection and service provision. Thus it provides the medium for the direct translation of uniform private property into public poverty and low levels of public service, without the hope of finding some resources in the taxes collected in more affluent sections of the jurisdiction. Table 4.1 presents representative data from upper-income white and lower-income black or racially mixed suburbs in the metropolitan areas of Chicago, Detroit, and Los Angeles.

We can see one feature of urban life in simple figures of racial segregation. The upper-income suburbs are virtually all white, ranging from 97.6 to 99.6 percent, whereas the lower-income suburbs are more heterogeneous in character. The Chicago suburbs of Harvey and Maywood, and the Detroit suburb of Inkster, combine lower-income white and black families with a majority of whites; the Detroit suburb of Highland Park, and the Los Angeles suburb of Compton, have black majorities with sizable white populations.

In all suburban comparisons, the affluent white suburbs have median family incomes about twice those in the lower-income suburbs, and have uniformly higher levels of education, lower unemployment rates, and crime rates ranging down to one-eighth as small. The incidence of families below the low-income level is only one-third to one-ninth that of the poorer suburbs, and the value of single-family, owner-occupied homes averages two to four times that in the poorer suburbs. In several communities these social and economic traits translate into tax revenues and local government expenditures that are higher in the affluent white suburbs, thus reinforcing with the weight of the public sector the differentials in standards of living that are already apparent in the private sector. One exception to this pattern occurs in the Detroit suburb of Highland Park, where an extensive manufacturing base helps provide the tax revenue to push local spending per capita higher than in the white enclaves of Birmingham and Southfield.

Table 4.1. Suburban Contrasts in Chicago, Detroit, and Los Angeles

	Percent White	Median Years Education of Adults	Median Family Income	Percent below Low-income Level	Median Value Owner-occupied Homes	Percent Unemployment	Serious Crimes per 1,000 Population	Property Taxes Per Capita	Current Government Expenditures Per Capita
Chicago:									
Highland Park	97.6	14.1	$20,844	2.1	$46,509	2.1	21.8	$ 48	$106
Northbrook	99.4	14.3	19,994	1.7	48,337	1.4	9.5	NA	NA
Wilmette	98.9	15.2	21,784	2.3	46,461	2.7	14.4	51	89
Harvey	68.8	11.7	11,329	7.0	17,117	3.8	72.5	26	69
Maywood	57.9	12.1	12,150	6.0	19,380	4.3	34.2	16	54
Detroit:									
Birmingham	99.6	14.1	17,297	2.1	31,736	2.6	20.9	95	152
Southfield	99.3	12.7	18,140	2.4	36,235	3.3	39.4	62	97
Highland Park	43.4	11.2	8,715	14.5	13,466	8.0	99.6	108	449
Inkster	55.2	11.7	11,280	8.4	17,242	6.2	78.6	44	93
Los Angeles:									
Beverly Hills	98.5	13.0	20,303	4.5	71,336	4.5	4.7	86	286
Compton	26.1	11.8	8,722	17.1	17,682	9.8	12.9	19	72

Source: County and City Data Book, 1972 (Washington, D.C.: U.S. Government Printing Office, 1973).

The Crisis in Urban Analysis

What results from these stark contrasts of urban wealth and poverty? You can choose from among widely differing analyses of the urban scene. Not only do points of view vary sharply, but usually with some bitterness. Intellectuals, politicians, and ordinary citizens feel strongly about urban affairs, and they are not above name-calling in reference to their adversaries. It is not too much of an exaggeration to say that the urban crisis in the United States is composed in equal parts of economic, social, political, and intellectual factors.

What some people say about the cities seems to fit their own needs on another stage. After the Watts riot in 1965, when President Lyndon B. Johnson was seeking popular support in the early phases of his war on poverty, he said: "The clock is ticking, time is moving ... we must ask ourselves every night when we go home, are we doing all that we should do in our nation's capital, in all the other big cities of the country?" [2] Almost eight years later, at the start of President Richard Nixon's second term, with the problems of Watergate already causing trouble and with this more conservative chief executive having an incentive to see improvements in the cities, he said: "A few years ago we constantly heard that urban America was on the brink of collapse. It was one minute to midnight, we were told.... Today, America is no longer coming apart.... The hour of crisis is past." [3]

The Unheavenly Reception of The Unheavenly City

Some commentaries on the cities have provoked crises of their own. The most prominent of these has been *The Un-*

2. Edward C. Banfield, *The Unheavenly City Revisited* (Boston: Little, Brown, 1974), p. 1.
3. Ibid., p. 1.

heavenly City: The Nature and Future of Our Urban Crisis by Edward C. Banfield, then a professor of government at Harvard University. The book was first published in 1970; by the time a revised version was published in 1974, the *Unheavenly City* had gone through twenty-two printings and had provoked intense debate and no little acrimony in government offices, mass-media talk shows, the professional journals of social science, and college campuses. By focusing on the arguments of Banfield and his critics, we see a wide range in the disputes about our cities. By using Banfield as the center of this discussion, however, we give somewhat more emphasis to the right wing of the discussion than its real proportion in all that has been written about the cities.

Banfield's analysis comes in four parts:

1. Sweeping allegations about an urban crisis fail to account for the tangible improvements in "material welfare."

> The plain fact is that the overwhelming majority of city dwellers live more comfortably and conveniently than ever before. They have more and better housing, more and better schools, more and better transportation, and so on.[4]

Banfield admits to serious problems for the poor and the blacks but these, too, are improving. "There is still much poverty and much racial discrimination. But there is less of both than ever before." [5]

2. We encounter many so-called problems of the cities by virtue of social and economic forces whose results, in the main, we applaud. Urban expansion, for example, is a corollary of population growth. The growth of surburbs—which excites both paeans of praise and words of condemnation from various

4. Ibid., p. 2.
5. Ibid.

observers—reflects technological developments (train, bus, and automobile) that make outward transportation feasible for large numbers of people. The suburban–central-city differentials in wealth reflect existing distributions of wealth that send to the outer suburbs those who can afford new housing and the time and money to commute, while keeping the "not well-off" in the older parts of the city.[6]

3. The real problems of the cities come more from emotional than from physical sources. This does not make the problems any easier to deal with. Indeed, the emotional sources of urban problems may make them even more difficult, given their elusive character and the failure of many people to recognize them.

Banfield sees two psychological dimensions in the urban crisis. The first is that much of the tension in the cities comes from people who feel themselves cut off from the mainstream, discriminated against, and not sharing in the general progress. As noted above, Banfield feels that tangible signs of progress appear throughout the city. Because expectations rise even faster than achievements, however, people at the lower end of the spectrum do not share this view of progress.

> To a large extent, then, our urban problems are like the mechanical rabbit at the racetrack, which is set to keep just ahead of the dogs no matter how fast they may run. Our performance is better and better, but because we set our standards and expectations to keep ahead of performance, the problems are never any nearer to solution. Indeed, if standards and expectations rise *faster* than performance, the problems may get (relatively) worse as they (absolutely) better.[7]

6. Ibid., p. 25.
7. Ibid., p. 24. Italics in original.

The second psychological dimension of the urban crisis appears in Banfield's conception of social classes. He defines classes not by objective measures of income, education, or occupation, but by individuals' "psychological orientation toward the future." [8] The problems of the cities are the problems of the *lower class*. Banfield takes pains to qualify his conception of the lower class, by noting that he describes an ideal type that may not appear in just these terms, and that he is not equating "lower class" with "Negro." Yet his definition of this class is stark, and it has brought him a great deal of criticism. He writes:

> ... the lower-class individual lives from moment to moment. If he has any awareness of a future, it is of something fixed, fated, beyond his control: things happen *to* him, he does not *make* them happen. Impulse governs his behavior, either because he cannot discipline himself to sacrifice a present for a future satisfaction or because he has no sense of the future. He is therefore radically improvident: whatever he cannot use immediately he considers valueless. His bodily needs (especially for sex) and his taste for "action" take precedence over everything else—and certainly over any work routine. He works only as he must to stay alive, and drifts from one unskilled job to another, taking no interest in his work.[9]

The existence of this lower class lies at the heart of the urban crisis:

> So long as the city contains a sizable lower class, nothing basic can be done about its most serious problems. Good

8. Ibid., p. 53.
9. Ibid., p. 61. Italics in original.

jobs may be offered to all, but some will remain chronically unemployed. Slums may be demolished, but if the housing that replaces them is occupied by the lower class it will shortly be turned into new slums. Welfare payments may be doubled or tripled and a negative income tax instituted, but some persons will continue to live in squalor and misery. New schools may be built, new curricula devised, and the teacher-pupil ratio cut in half, but if the children who attend these schools come from lower-class homes, the schools will be turned into blackboard jungles, and those who graduate or drop out from them will, in most cases, be functionally illiterate. The streets may be filled with armies of policemen, but violent crimes and civil disorder will decrease very little.[10]

4. Because few commentators and policy makers separate the tangible and the psychological dimensions of urban affairs, the programs designed and implemented in the cities do not fit the need. Some programs are not directed at the poor but at the affluent, and actually add to the problems of the poor. Banfield finds that urban renewal intensifies the housing problems of the poor; and highway construction facilitates the exodus of affluent residents and businesses from the central city, thus leaving fewer jobs and more segregated neighborhoods.[11]

Other problems come from those who fail to see the impediments resulting from the psychological traits of the lower class, and who blame the urban crisis on the failure of the white population to rid itself of racism or to provide tangible benefits to the poor. To Banfield, this self-delusion and self-debasement on the part of middle- and upper-class whites spreads the sense of failure and discrimination throughout the

10. Ibid., pp. 234–35.
11. Ibid., pp. 14–16.

community and increases the likelihood that large concentrations of lower-class blacks, feeling themselves permanently kept out of the mainstream, will seek outlets in destructive ways.

These psychological dimensions of the urban crisis have a special significance for the theme of this book. Because the United States is both a developed and a developing country, it has great resources to spend for the material improvements required by urban residents. To the extent that basic needs are emotional and not material, however, these financial resources will have only limited utility. We have proved our ability to build roads, buildings, and elaborate equipment. We have been less successful in operating social services to meet the complex demands of needy people.

Banfield has earned the label *iconoclast* by his consideration of several policy alternatives that seem "feasible" in being constitutional and capable of achieving desired goals, but not "acceptable" to important sectors of the community. His proposals include:

a. Avoiding rhetoric that would raise expectations beyond the point where society could deliver, or would encourage the individual to believe that society and not himself is responsible for his problems
b. Repealing minimum-wage laws, and ceasing to overpay for low-skilled employment
c. Reducing the school-leaving age to fourteen
d. Redefining poverty in terms of nearly fixed standards of hardship rather than standards of relative deprivation that tend to escalate continuously
e. Encouraging "problem" families to send children to day nurseries and preschools designed to bring children into contact with non-lower-class culture
f. Abridging the freedom of those who—in the

opinion of a court—are "extremely likely to commit
violent crimes"

g. Prohibiting "live" television coverage of riots.[12]

Banfield is inclined to let certain "natural" forces alleviate
urban problems rather than give their solution to policy
makers who do not see the psychological dynamics of the
urban scene. "That government cannot solve the problems of
the cities and is likely to make them worse by trying does not
necessarily mean that calamity impends." [13] Banfield's hopes
focus on economic growth, which will provide continuing
relief for the tangible needs of the cities' populations; demographic changes, which will alleviate population pressures
some years after declining birthrates; and the gradual
processes of "middle- and upper-class-ification" that will absorb members of the lower class into the outlook and life styles
of the mainstream.[14]

Professor Banfield has not received gentle treatment.
Distinguished fellow political scientists have called his work
"racism," "fascism," and "primative conservatism." Former
Mayor Carl Stokes of Cleveland finds the book a "controver-
sial piece of urban fiction." The titles of review articles provide
some flavor of the reception: "Patent Racism," "Survival of
the Fattest," "The City as Purgatory," "Class, Race, and
Reaction: A Trivial but Dangerous Analysis."

Some of the negative reviews tell as much about the critics' ideology as they do about Banfield's book. These also
demonstrate views of urban crisis that lie at the opposite end of
the spectrum from Banfield. Professor Robert E. Agger, writing from McMaster University in Ontario, limits his praise to
Banfield's "making a forthright statement . . . that socio-eco-

12. Ibid., pp. 269–70.
13. Ibid., p. 281.
14. Ibid., pp. 281–82.

nomic-cultural class is the name of the most important game in the United States, especially in the big cities and metropoli of that country." [15] Once that compliment is out, Agger goes on to cite Banfield for "monstrous ideology . . . a prescription for American fascism . . . a persuasive call to silence, or at most only mild dissent, in the face of increasing national repression and suppression of those who continue to insist on reformation or disintegration of the new medieval fortresses (whether luxury high rises or suburban castles) of the American cities." [16] Agger sees Banfield's book to be dangerous in Canada as well as the United States. "There are Canadians, as well as colonial administrators of branch plants of numerous American multinational corporations . . . who may find *The Unheavenly City* exactly what they were looking for . . . a view of urban problems that . . . can lead to temporarily increased domestic peace and quiet and a final solution in the form of a brutalized—albeit 'high educated'—citizenry and the new fascism of the post-industrial, scientific-technological world." [17]

In more temperate passages, several of Banfield's reviewers have called attention to the psychological view of social classes that is central to his analysis. Some find this view receiving too little documentation in Banfield's book and too little support in the research of other social scientists. A prominent economist finds that Banfield exaggerates the constraints imposed by traits of the lower class on policy-makers' ability to bring about economic changes in the cities.[18] Some reviewers feel that Banfield makes it too easy for a reader to slip from the concept *lower class* to *Negroes,* and that he lends

15. Robert E. Agger, "Class, Race and Reaction: A Trivial but Dangerous Analysis," *Social Science Quarterly* 51 (March 1971): 835.

16. Ibid., p. 836.

17. Ibid., p. 852. See also Duane Lockard, "Patent Racism," *Trans-action* 8 (March/April 1971): 69–72.

18. Robert Lampman, "Moral Realism and the Poverty Question," *Social Science Quarterly* 51 (March 1971): 830–34.

weight to the troublesome element of white racism. Carl Stokes expresses the view of several commentators when he cites Banfield's preoccupation with social statistics, and his lack of feeling for the plight of the poor and the blacks who find themselves in hopeless situations.[19] Yet this attachment to feelings is what Banfield finds wrong in many politicians and social commentators. The excess weighting of feelings over facts, in his view, produces the "reign of error" that can make matters worse in the face of much activity designed to "do good."[20]

The Unwalled City

Another view of American cities comes from Norton E. Long. His comments are helpful because, like Banfield's, they require us to go beyond the tangible needs that elicit responses from the great productivity of the United States economy. The full title of Long's book summarizes its message: *The Unwalled City: Reconstituting the Urban Community.* In Long's view, the city suffers from the loss of its inhabitants' sense of attachment to a community. They are residents and no longer *citizens.* They scatter homes and jobs throughout the several jurisdictions of the metropolitan area and view the city in opportunistic terms: as a place to work, find entertainment, shop, and perhaps live. This attitude affects city employees as well as inhabitants. Indeed, the bureaucrats are the greatest scourge in Long's analysis. They are "centralized, irresponsible, and unresponsive"; their behavior is "stagnant, costly, unenterprising, consumer-be-damned."[21] "The most important, the best organized, the most concerned, and the most destructive of the city are the public employees and their unions."[22]

19. Carl Stokes, "The Poor Need Not Always Be With Us," *Social Science Quarterly* 51 (March 1971): 821–26.
20. Banfield, *Unheavenly City Revisited,* pp. 274, 283.
21. Norton E. Long, *The Unwalled City: Reconstituting the Urban Community* (New York: Basic, 1972), p. 93.
22. Ibid., p. 187.

At various points in his book, Long contrasts the amoral city with communities that benefit from intense member attachment: an Amish schoolhouse, the State of Israel, and Black Muslims. These produce more outputs to their members with less resources than can be found in the input-output ratios of American cities. He likens the cities to the railways. He does not make the analogy clear but seems to have in mind the cities' exploitation by all concerned, and foremost their employees, with no effort to maintain a capital structure that will keep the system viable from one generation to the next. Elsewhere he characterizes the cities as Indian reservations: highly dependent on outsiders and subsidized by a "welfare colonialism" that may prevent starvation but creates additional problems (e.g., subsidizing broken families). Yet another analogy has particular interest for our view that the United States bears several marks of a developing country:

Many a newcomer, coming from a peasant culture such as southern Italy, would see the state from the perspective shown in *Christ Stopped in Eboli,* as a hostile force that taxed the harvests, took sons for the army, and gave nothing in return. The American state and its visible embodiment, the city, might seem a great improvement, not because it did much but because it left him with more of what could be made in a prosperous society. The apathy toward local government on the part of the lower classes has not been the result of a conviction of the triviality of city hall—witness the expression "you can't beat city hall"—but a feeling that the best you could hope for was to be let alone or, if lucky, to make something personally out of an "in" with the bosses.[23]

23. Ibid., pp. 122–23.

Structural Impediments to Urban Problem Solving

Whether the sources of urban difficulties appear in root causes of economics, culture, or psychology, a common thread in many analyses leads to the dualism of affluence and poverty, white and black. Despite the huge resources of the United States, this country is still a long way from the equality in economic or social conditions that prevails in some other countries of the world or—within this country—in some of the states. In urban areas, a special problem is that economic resources are separated by local government boundaries from the sites having the greatest needs. Borders between neighboring cities, counties, suburban towns, school districts, and special districts divide an urban area into a surplus of jurisdictions. Often they compete with one another to keep taxes low. Some local jurisdictions have a greater tax base than required to support their services, so their levies 'can be low. Other jurisdictions—like central cities and poor suburbs—have needs that surpass their resources. They may raise taxes to the legal or political limits, but untapped resources remain in neighboring jurisdictions.

State constitutions and statutes add to the problems of urban governments by limiting the kinds of taxes they can raise. Restrictions keep most localities to the regressive and unpopular tax on the real property that lies within their borders. The regressive nature of this tax restrains its contribution to local treasuries during periods of inflation; tax rates do not move automatically higher with inflation, as they do in the case of progressive federal and state income taxes. The unpopularity of the property tax dampens the frequent increases in rates or assessments that are needed to keep revenues up to increases in prices and service demands. And restrictions to a tax on locally situated property keep the cities from tapping much of the economic resources (e.g., the incomes and retail purchases of suburbanites) centered in the urban area.

Policy controversies have been especially sharp over the subject of equal support for public education in neighboring jurisdictions. In Los Angeles County, for example, the tax base of Beverly Hills is $50,885 per pupil, while nearby Baldwin Park's is $3,706. As a result, a 13.7 percent property tax levy would be required in Baldwin Park to collect the same revenue that Beverly Hills would receive from a 1 percent tax.[24]

Suits have been filed in several courts, charging that school financing such as this violates the equal protection clause of the Fourteenth Amendment to the United States Constitution. Existing arrangements are said to allow "wide variations in the expenditures per student from district to district, thereby providing some students with a good education and depriving others, who have equal or greater educational needs." [25] During 1973, however, in *Rodriquez* v. *San Antonio Independent School District*, the United States Supreme Court ruled against this argument by a 5–4 vote. Although this decision represents a setback for proponents of school-finance reform, the close vote of the Court and hopes for an ultimate reversal will keep the issue alive.

A Frustrated Reform Movement

The first major response to the problem of surplus jurisdictions in metropolitan areas and their segregation of resources from needs came during the 1950s and 1960s. It sought to integrate the separate jurisdictions by any of several approaches:[26]

24. Robert D. Reischauer and Robert W. Hartman, *Reforming School Finance* (Washington, D.C.: Brookings, 1973), p. 32.

25. Ibid., p. 58.

26. This section relies on Lineberry and Sharkansky, *Urban Politics,* pp. 128–34.

1. Municipal regulation of real estate developments in the rural fringe outside its borders
2. Development of metropolitan-wide districts
3. Annexation and city-city consolidation
4. Consolidation of the city with the urbanized county surrounding it
5. Federation of several municipalities

Few of these reform efforts were successful. Voters tended to be apathetic, and most established elites were hostile. Officials of local governments, political party chiefs, leaders of unions, and the black community were accustomed to the existing structures in which they had come to power and feared dilution of their political bases in any aggregation of diverse communities.

Out of 47 referenda on metropolitan reorganization undertaken in 36 of the nation's 212 Standard Metropolitan Statistical Areas during 1946-68, only 18 produced favorable votes. Even this figure overstates the success of reform efforts. It reports only those campaigns where reform tickets were strong enough to put the issue on the ballot. Also, few major reforms occurred in the largest metropolitan areas.

For most of the postwar period, the more prominent movement in metropolitan areas created *more rather than fewer* jurisdictions. Between 1952 and 1972, the number of local government units other than school districts increased by 13,036. This was largely a result of continued suburban development, but the growth also affected sentiments in the metropolitan core. The central-city movements had several names: *decentralization, neighborhood control, community control, control-sharing*. Some arrangements would actually decentralize the power to make program decisions, and others would merely provide representation on a centralized policy-making body to program clients. All such arrangements would further complicate the task of financing services in urban areas, with many problems focused on the issue of who would pay for the services provided the residents of inner-city communities.

Most efforts at decentralization occurred in black ghettos, but any explanation of the move toward additional governments within central cities must take account of the earlier blossoming of suburban units. Spokesmen for inner-city decentralization justified their demands by reference to the suburbs. Ghetto leaders wanted for themselves the benefits of local autonomy.

The Role of State and Federal Aid

With the failure of metropolitan interpretation to rationalize local government boundaries, the taxing and spending powers of state and national governments came to the fore. State and national governments collect taxes throughout a metropolitan area, regardless of municipal borders. Moreover, their levies on personal incomes are progressive, and—as tax rates automatically move upward with incomes—they help to keep revenue collections ahead of prices during inflation. It is the good fortune of American cities to suffer their lagged development amid a wealthy economy.

In recent years, both state and national governments have increased their financing of local services. Moreover, state and national aids are going increasingly to local governments with the largest populations and, presumably, the most difficult social and economic problems. In the largest cities (over 500,000 population), 43.5 percent of expenditures come initially from Washington and state capitals. For all other cities, the percentage received as aid is 33.5. Since the most dramatic takeoff in new social programs in the 1964–65 period, the largest cities' per capita receipts of intergovernmental aid have grown by 329 percent, while those of other cities have grown by 263 percent.

There has been a growing federal role in local (and state) finance since 1961. Federal aid as a percentage of state and local government expenditures increased from 12.6 in the last budget of the Eisenhower administration to 23.8 in 1973. For fiscal year 1974, the Nixon administration proposed a halt in growth that would bring federal contributions down to 21.3 percent of state and local expenditures. Watergate complicated the President's relations with Congress, however, and large segments of his proposal did not emerge from committee rooms.

State governments also deserve credit for their awareness of urban affairs. Cities over 500,000 population received $2.2 billion from the national government during 1972–73, but $5.9 billion from the states. Admittedly, some unknown portion of the states' $5.9 billion came initially from Washington. Like the national government, the states are giving the greatest aid to the largest cities, and are increasing most the aid to those cities. From 1964–65 to 1972–73 state aid per capita to cities over 500,000 population increased by 270 percent, while per capita state aid to other cities increased by 211 percent.

In recent years state governments have loosened their controls over local finances. Local governments in eleven states now collect income taxes, and local governments in twenty-six states collect sales taxes. Through these devices, central cities can tap the pockets of suburbanites who work or shop within their borders.

The combined effects of more generous state and national aid plus fewer state restrictions on local finance help direct a greater share of the country's public resources toward urban problems. Big-cities' expenditures increased by some 171 percent over the period 1964 to 1972–73, while those of all other domestic units of government increased by 122 percent. Moreover, some of the 122 percent increase has occurred in state and national budgets that support their own programs in large cities: social security pensions, veterans hospitals, and urban campuses of state universities.

American Cities in International Comparison

How close is the resemblance between the cities of the United States and those of Africa, Asia, and Latin America? In what respects do our cities fit the image of the United States as a developing country? In certain respects, the fit is close. In the United States as in the poor countries, cities feel the greatest impact of social and economic change. Much of this change is threatening. In the large cities of the United States and else-where, violence can wreck orderly processes of government. The United States and most poor countries are becoming increasingly urban, and these movements are contrary to much of what is prized in the various national myths. The United States is now more urban than most poor countries, but the poor countries are urbanizing at a more rapid rate.

In most respects that can be defined precisely and made subject to hard measurements, the cities of poor countries are even less well off than those of the United States. Rates of urban population growth are considerably higher in the poor countries: urban areas grow at twice the rate of national population throughout Africa. In the United States metropolitan growth was only 2.4 percent greater than the national rate in 1960–70.[27] Moreover, American cities rest on a wealthier economy. Urbanologists who study poor countries have adopted the term *macrocephaly* to convey the image of cities that have ballooned far out of proportion to the rest of the country. The analogy is drawn to the oversized head of a

27. Colin Rosser, "Urbanization in Tropical Africa: A Demographic Introduction" (Working Papers of the International Urbanization Survey, Ford Foundation, New York), p. 36.

dwarf. Whereas the United States has some 153 cities with more than 100,000 population, the pattern in poor countries is to have one large city or a very small number of them. In Peru, for example, some 20 percent of the population lives in or around Lima, and the next-largest city has but one-fifteenth of Lima's population.[28]

Many cities in poor countries also lie closer to the edge of minimum order than do American cities. With a continuing influx of school leavers from rural areas creating uncounted unemployment, and with primitive housing sprouting up in unregulated fashion to provide basic shelter, rudimentary city administrations seem hardly able to cope.

> In Metropolitan Lagos, for example, chaotic traffic conditions have become endemic; demands on the water supply system have begun to outstrip its maximum capacity; power cuts have become chronic as industrial and domestic requirements have escalated; factories have been compelled to bore their own wells and to set up stand-by electricity plants; public transport has been inundated; port facilities have been stretched to their limits . . . and city government has threatened to break down amidst charges of corruption, mismanagement and financial incompetence.[29]

A common response to excessive urbanization in the poor countries is national planning in behalf of "rural development." This takes different forms and is motivated by various drives. Some motives are humanitarian: to provide improved standards of living for the rural poor who continue to make up a majority of the population, and whose opportunities in rural

28. John P. Robin and Frederick C. Terzo, "Urbanization in Peru," Working Papers, pp. ii–iii.
29. Leslie Green and Vincent Milone, "Urbanization in Nigeria: A Planning Commentary," Working Papers, pp. 14–15.

areas remain substantially less than in the cities. Some motives are short range and ad hoc in their efforts to stem a great urban flow of unskilled peasants destined to be frustrated in their search for jobs. In Kenya, for example, a study done in the mid-1960s found 148,000 students completing primary school during one year; 92,000 had no prospect of further education, and only 3,500 of these could find urban wage employment. Since then, the number of primary school leavers has grown, and the number of places in secondary schools has not kept pace. An even larger number of young people seek jobs in urban areas each year, with the overwhelming majority of them destined to fail.[30]

Other motives for national planning in behalf of rural areas are more long range in their perspectives: to take advantage of the lesser investment required to create new jobs in agriculture than in urban industry, and to spur the production of raw materials that bring foreign exchange in world markets. This strategy concedes that urban manufacturers in the poor countries are not likely to sell profitably in foreign commerce and will require subsidies even to survive in domestic markets.

There is some desperation in the efforts of poor countries to encourage economic growth in their rural areas. The natural growth of population, industry, and commerce has taken place in the cities where, despite their problems, there are ready benefits of transportation arteries, electric power, a water supply, and the best aggregation of skills and capital available to the country. It is not a simple task to redirect growth. It requires government to assemble a package of incentives or controls to outweigh the free-market incentives that lure individuals and business firms to the big city. Insofar as private investment continues in the big cities, urban unemployment may increase even faster than the jobs because new jobs attract

30. John Gerhart, "Urbanization in Kenya: Rural Development and Urban Growth," Working Papers, p. 6.

several times their number of new rural migrants.[31] Government effectiveness is not the strong suit of most poor countries. Too few civil servants can resist the temptations put in their way by businessmen seeking exceptions to controls. Indeed, few civil servants are themselves willing to leave the benefits of the capital in order to pursue their careers in provincial towns.

There is an acceptance of continued urban expansion among some writers who deal with the cities of poor countries, despite the problems of crowding, inadequate services, and the nasty aesthetics of poverty and sprawl. Writing about the squatter settlements in and around large cities, revisionists see them as natural results of economic incentives drawing people to cities that cannot accommodate them according to the wishes of conventional planners and middle-class citizens. In this view, the new settlers make do with rudiments of housing, water, and sanitation—equivalent to what they had known in rural areas; their slum settlements offer proximity to the central-city's employment opportunities; and rather than being the habitat of criminals and misfits, their settlements contain stable families that improve their standards of living as incomes permit.[32] This view of squatter settlements in poor countries bears some resemblance to Banfield's view of American cities: both take another look at living conditions that earlier reformers had perceived as ugly and intolerable, and both find the conditions to be acceptable manifestations of ongoing economic forces.

Conclusion

It may be stretching things to compare contemporary cities of the United States with those of Africa, Asia, and Latin Amer-

31. Ibid., p. 2.
32. Robin and Terzo, "Urbanization in Peru," pp. 9–13.

ica. The problems of New York and Detroit are not those of Calcutta or Lagos, no matter how bad things may seem in the United States. Yet America's cities—or at least several aspects of many cities—bear a significant resemblance to cities in poor countries. Urban dualism in the United States—between rich and poor, white and black—is severe. On the single dimension of crime, the cities of America require special consideration. To the extent that violent crimes reflect urban social tensions and the cities' lack of a settled character, then the cities of the United States stand as less developed than those of most other affluent countries.

Edward Banfield, Norton Long, and others make the important point that lavish spending on public buildings, welfare payments, and social services do not assure a solution to our urban problems. Psychological components of those problems confound simple treatments and turn serious efforts at analysis—e.g., Banfield's—into provocative elements of the urban crisis. However, the financial and personnel resources available to our cities take at least some of the edge off their problems. Our cities receive large and increasing investments of public resources. Expenditures on urban social services are growing faster than population or inflation. Starting from a new awareness of urban problems in the mid-1960s, and continuing through the first term of the Nixon administration, public expenditures per capita in cities with populations over 500,000 grew by some 72 percent in constant dollars.[33] In this as in other cases, those sectors of the United States that resemble the developing countries benefit from their setting amid the wealth of a developed country.

33. *City Government Finances in the United States, 1964–65* and *1971–72* (Washington. D.C.: U.S. Government Printing Office. 1966, 1973).

5

☆ _____

RACIAL DUALISM

Lurking behind each comparison made so far between the United States and the poor countries of Africa, Asia, and Latin America has been the subject of race. The contrasts between rich and poor sectors of the United States that have received widespread attention are those between whites and blacks. Not all of America's poor are black, and not all its affluent are white. Yet the single trait that is most prominently related to poverty is race. Most states that rank low on measures of economic development have large black populations. Most large cities with severe urban problems have large black populations; further, many discussions about the problems of these cities focus on the black ghettos and their poverty, drug addiction, school dropout rate, unemployment, poor housing, and political tension.

Any effort to understand the underdeveloped character of the United States must pursue a frontal attack on the racial question. Are the developmental problems of the United States simply "black" problems? The answer is no. Nevertheless, the overlap between racial dualism and the other dualisms treated in this book is sufficiently close to require careful examination. This chapter looks at racial contrasts in the United States and shows how they add to our comprehension of developmental features in the United States. Our racial contrasts and conflicts have their parallels in the poor countries. Many of their political features, like ours, derive from ethnic and economic overlappings whereby certain ethnic or racial groups get the short end of the stick in incomes, social status, political power, and benefits from public services. As we have seen in other chapters, however, the contrasts between affluence and poverty in the United States exist amid aggregate resources that are the greatest in the world. These resources must be considered in a discussion of racial dualism in the United States, because they go a long way toward ameliorating the conditions of our disadvantaged population.

Racial Dualism in the United States

Anyone who has read this far need not be reminded of the contrasts in economic, social, and political characteristics of blacks and whites in the United States. Indeed, anyone sufficiently interested in public affairs even to notice the title of this book has undoubtedly seen many prior references to racial contrasts. Of all the dualisms to be found in this country, racial dualism receives most of the attention from the mass media, social scientists, and politicians.

Why all the attention to differences between blacks and white? The answer is *not* that these are the sharpest differences. Data on incomes and schooling indicate differences between Anglos and Spanish-origin people almost as sharp or sharper than between those for whites and blacks. Information about Indian incomes and education is not as plentiful or as reliable as for the larger ethnic blocs, but indications are that Native Americans show the *lowest* scores on economic and educational traits. Some idea of the differentials between blacks and Indians come from "nonwhite" infant death rates by state. Nonwhite infant death rates for Mississippi, Alabama, Georgia, and the Carolinas range from 37 to 48 per 1,000 live births, and in these states blacks outnumber other nonwhite groups by more than 10 to 1. In Utah and Wyoming, nonwhite infant death rates are 52 and 56 per 1,000 live births, and in these states the incidence of Indians exceeds blacks by about 2 to 1.

The sheer number of blacks, their increasing concentration in our largest cities, and the quality of their political organization explains the prominence of the black-white contrasts in public affairs. The 1970 Census recorded 22.6 million blacks, approximately 11 percent of the population. Since 1950, the black population has increased by 51 percent, but the black population in central cities of metropolitan areas has increased by 99 percent. Consider some racial data for fifty-seven cities with over 250,000 population. Blacks comprise at least 20 percent of the population in twenty-six of these cities. and are a majority in three (Atlanta, Newark, and Washington). Nationwide, the ethnic groups that compete with blacks for the lowest rungs on the economic and political ladders do not approach the blacks in number: there are only 9 million Spanish-origin people and some 793,000 Indians. Also, these groups are not as concentrated as blacks in politically sensitive cities and are not as well organized by ethnic political leaders.

We must guard against the simple conclusion that blacks are the poorest sector of the population. We must also realize that the incidence of blacks in large cities and in low-income states does not by itself produce the dualism cited for those states and cities in the previous chapters. Statistics for blacks do not account for all the poverty in the less-developed states or the large cities. Far from it. The low-income states of the South have large numbers of poor whites as well as poor blacks. The large metropolitan areas have poor white ghettos in their central cities, as well as poor white suburbs. Table 5.1

shows the incidence of the total population and the incidence of blacks living below the "low income" lines in the lowest-income states and in those cities with over 250,000 population having at least 20 percent black population. Where a state or city has an incidence of blacks below the low-income line that is greater than the national incidence of poor people, it is likely to have a disproportionate incidence of poor whites as well. Recall the discussion in the previous chapter. There it was noted that "black" suburbs are not homogeneously black but contain low-income whites along with large pluralities—or majorities—of blacks.

Table 5.1. **Incidence of Low-Income Families, by Race, Selected States and Cities, 1969**

| | Percent Below Low-Income Levels | |
	Total Population	*Blacks*
States		
Alabama	20.7	46.8
Arkansas	22.9	53.0
Kentucky	19.3	33.5
Louisiana	21.6	47.6
Mississippi	29.0	54.4
New Mexico	18.6	34.4
North Carolina	16.5	39.0
South Carolina	18.1	45.0
Tennessee	18.3	38.1
West Virginia	18.1	32.1
Cities		
Atlanta	15.9	25.1
Baltimore	14.0	23.2
Birmingham	17.4	34.3
Buffalo	11.2	24.4
Chicago	10.6	20.7
Cincinnati	12.8	26.6
Cleveland	13.5	23.3
Dallas	10.1	25.1
Detroit	11.3	18.7

Table 5.1. (continued)

Cities	Total Population	Blacks
Houston	10.7	25.3
Jacksonville	14.1	34.8
Jersey City	10.3	19.5
Kansas City, Mo.	8.9	20.5
Louisville	13.0	28.7
Memphis	15.7	35.7
Miami	16.4	27.9
New Orleans	21.6	38.9
New York	11.5	20.5
Newark	18.4	23.6
Norfolk	16.1	33.9
Oakland	12.2	21.8
Philadelphia	11.2	21.4
Pittsburgh	11.2	26.9
Richmond	13.3	24.7
Saint Louis	14.4	25.5
Washington, D.C.	12.7	15.5
United States	10.7	32.2

Source: *County and City Data Book, 1972* (Washington, D.C.: U.S. Government Printing Office, 1973).

Thus it is wrong to equate *black* and *poor* in the United States as a whole, in its less-developed states, or in its large cities. Despite this, however, the black population remains the one sector most commanding of study from our perspective of the United States as a developing country. This focus on blacks results from their larger number than other depressed groups, from their concentration in important cities, and from the quality of their political organization. The focus on blacks also results from the wealth of social science literature on them. More than in the case of Spanish-origin people or Indians, we can draw upon the findings of demography, economics, opinion research, and political analysis to document the character of black-white dualism in the United States. Drawing from this literature, the following sections show how our black and white "nations" differ from one another, and how these differences parallel dualisms in the poor countries of Africa, Asia, and Latin America. With this information, we should take a considerable step toward understanding the payoffs associated with viewing the United States as a developing country.

The Black Nation within the United States

Professor Matthew Holden begins a discussion of black politics by referring to *Sybil,* a widely read novel by Benjamin Disraeli, which focused on the two nations of rich and poor in nineteenth-century England. In Holden's persuasive argument, a close parallel exists between Disraeli's setting and present black-white relations in the United States.[1] Both black and white live within the common legal framework of the United States. Yet they differ so

> significantly as to physical places of residence, cultural
> styles and outlooks, levels of capital and income,
> political habits, legal rights, and habits of
> communication and exchange, then it may be quite
> reasonable to describe them as separate "nations." [2]

For purposes of this book, the important traits of the black nation are its culture, economy, and government. With distinctive attributes on each of these features, American blacks portray the multiplicity of distinctions that other peoples have cited for their own nationhood. To call a people a nation, of course, is not to bestow statehood upon them. American blacks exhibit the traits of a distinct nation within a larger state. In this

1. Matthew Holden, Jr., *The Politics of the Black Nation* (New York: Chandler, 1973), p. 1.
2. Ibid.

they resemble such people as the French in Canada, the Scots and Welsh in the United Kingdom, the Basques in Spain, the Ibo in Nigeria, and the Luo in Kenya. American blacks lack an obviously distinct language to set them apart. This lack traces itself to the forced integration of slavery. Linguists find distinct patterns in the speech of American blacks, however, and have begun some efforts to employ black dialect in reading classes of ghetto schools.

The awareness of a black nation within the United States has several implications. For this book's theme of dualism, the message is clear: the American black nation differs in culture, economics, and politics from the prevailing patterns, and on each of these traits the black nation has a subordinate position. Many black people feel themselves inhabitants of our domestic colony, exploited in the same way as subordinate nationalities in the poor countries. For policy makers, the recognition of a distinct black culture, economy, and polity has meaning for the design of public services, and for efforts to communicate effectively with black citizens and with black members of the government bureaucracy. To a substantial degree, this recognition exists. Human-relations programs appear in military and civilian agencies of the national government and in numerous states and localities. They seek to make black and white officials aware of one another's traits, and to facilitate white officials' communications with black clients. Increasingly well organized groups of black professionals, politicians, and businessmen seek to educate white elites about the policy demands of the black community. It is not fashionable to describe American blacks as members of a nation. In popular discourse, the term "black community" is less provocative but carries much of the same meaning as Holden's "nation."

Black Culture
Holden identifies several themes in the culture of black Americans that have relevance for politics. The themes are not

without their anomalies and sharp tensions between seemingly contrary features. This is to be expected. The black nation is large and diverse, and its political culture does not reduce to simple statements. Neither, of course, does the political culture of white Americans.

One set of traits that exists in the black culture, according to Holden, is the *hope for deliverance* and the *wish for defiance.* As in other traits that Holden describes, these presume the larger existence of cultural conflict between whites and blacks, with the whites on top. Holden writes, "White supremacy is the single most important fact in the *environment* of black politics." [3] Elsewhere he softens the concept of "white supremacy" with the statement that "the white element has been *dominant* over the black element." [4] *Deliverance,* then, refers to a hoped-for end to the suffering that comes along with subordination. *Defiance* stands as the aggressive pursuit of that deliverance, in contrast with the passive hope for help. Rather than "God will deliver us someday," the theme of defiance is "telling the white man where to go and what to do, and making him go and do it!" [5]

Holden also finds *Dionysian individualism* in the black culture. This is comprised of several items, each seeming to have some connection with the superior-subordinate position of the two nations and the postures that individual blacks take with regard to pervasive challenges against their self-esteem. One Dionysian trait is the swagger of young black males; another is the rich oratory of black preachers and politicians; another is the tendency for black leaders to run their organizations in an authoritarian style. Perhaps related to all these traits is a tendency for frequent segmentation and secession within black organizations. This permits the maximum expression of Dionysian individualism, by allowing for the expres-

3. Ibid., p. 42.
4. Ibid., p. 213. Italics in original.
5. Ibid., pp. 18–19.

sion of one's own sense of honor without the encumbrance of a hostile organization.

Yet another trait in black culture, as Holden sees it, is *moralistic discourse.* This may be a simple residue from conservative Protestant religious bodies, or it may be yet another link to the blacks' subordination and dependence on outside forces. But lest we think too much of the blacks as willing to rely on others, there is also the trait of *cynicism:* the realization that others are not likely to pursue the best interest of blacks without a good deal of prodding.

We can find in the results of opinion research some further indications of black and white "nations," and evidence for the specific elements that Holden identifies with the black culture. Table 5.2 reports several polls that reveal black and white differences with respect to such general feelings as contentment, views toward forces outside oneself, and trust. They show less satisfaction among blacks than whites with respect to the quality of housing, work, income, children's education, and—most generally—"the quality of life in your community." The polls also show, and not surprisingly, that blacks are less "happy" than whites, are more likely to see their lives as "dull" rather than "exciting," and are more likely to see success coming from "luck" as opposed to "ability" (a sign, perhaps, of Holden's expression of dependence on outside forces).

The desires of blacks with respect to public services also differ from those of whites. Again, the differences should not surprise anyone with the remotest acquaintance with American society and economics, but the differences do point to the penetration of these conditions into the opinions found within the black nation. Blacks, more than whites, support school busing to achieve racial integration; blacks are more likely to feel that desegration has been too slow; blacks are more likely to support such things as government-provided day-care centers for working mothers, a guaranteed annual income, and financial restitution to the black community for historic injus-

Table 5.2. **Public-Opinion Poll Showing General Feelings, by Race**

	Whites	*Blacks*
On the whole, would you say you are satisfied or dissatisfied with the work you do? (March-April 1969)		
Satisfied	88%	76%
Dissatisfied	6	18
No opinion	6	6
On the whole, would you say you are satisfied or dissatisfied with your family income? (March-April 1969)		
Satisfied	67	44
Dissatisfied	30	54
No opinion	3	2
On the whole, would you say you are satisfied or dissatisfied with your housing situation? (March-April 1969)		
Satisfied	80	50
Dissatisfied	18	48
No opinion	2	2
In general, how happy would you say you are—very happy, fairly happy, or not happy? (December 1970)[a]		
Very	46	20
Fairly	46	63
Not happy	5	12
No answer	3	5
In general, do you find life exciting, pretty routing, or dull? (September 1969)		
Exciting	49	31
Routine, dull	49	63
No opinion	2	6
Do you think people who are successful get ahead largely because of their luck or largely because of their ability? (April 1970)		
Luck	7	15
Ability	87	82
No opinion	6	3

[a] Respondents to this question were labeled "whites" and "nonwhites."
Source: The Gallup Poll: Public Opinion 1935-71 (New York: Random House, 1972), vol. 3.

tices. And when blacks and whites are asked to identify national problems that should receive government attention, blacks are the more likely to emphasize tangible items that affect them directly as poor people who are subject to deprivations and discrimination: housing, the needs of people in poor areas, and racial discrimination. Whites' lists of national problems are more likely to feature generally perceived national needs, as opposed to a relief of tangible burdens directly experienced: crime, air and water pollution, and public education.

In many sectors of public life in the United States there are direct clashes between the races. These occur over busing and other features of school integration, where the racial issues are out front; and on such matters as housing, income policy, and crime, where race lurks right beneath the surface. As we see, in table 5.3, there are racial differences in attitudes toward each of these policy areas.

Other racial differences appear in their members' trust in government. Table 5.4 comes from an opinion survey in Detroit. Here is evidence for Holden's notion of black cynicism. The surveys portray less black trust in both federal and local governments, and especially low black regard for the local police.

One element that gives special value to opinion studies of Detroit is its history of racial tension. The latest major episode came in 1968 and stands—together with Newark, Cleveland, and Watts—as among the bloodiest in our 1965–68 era of racial explosion. One set of questions asking blacks and whites about the reasons for the disorders is especially revealing of the different cultural perspectives. Table 5.5 shows that blacks are more likely to ascribe the disorders to people being treated badly, while whites ascribe riots to "criminals" and "people [who] wanted to take things." Indeed, here we see the sharpest of the attitudinal differences in tables 5.2 through 5.5: a clear majority of whites see the riots resulting from criminal elements within the black community, while a clear majority of

Table 5.3. **Public Opinion Poll With Respect to Public Services, by Race**

	Whites	Blacks
What is your opinion—do you think the racial intergration of schools in the United States is going too fast or not fast enough? (July 1969)		
Too fast	46%	20%
Not fast enough	20	45
About right	27	24
No opinion	8	10
Day-care centers for very young children are being set up so that mothers living in poor areas can take jobs and so that the children can get early educational training. How do you feel about this—would you favor or oppose having the federal government provide funds to set up these centers in most communities? (June 1969)		
Favor	63	83
Oppose	32	11
No opinion	5	6
A Negro organization is asking American churches and synagogues to pay $500 million to Negroes because of past injustices. How do you feel about this—would you favor or oppose this being done? (May 1969)		
Favor	2	21
Oppose	94	52
No opinion	4	27
As you may know, there is talk about guaranteeing every family an income of at least $3,200 a year, which would be the amount for a family of four. If the family earns less than this, the government would make up the difference. Would you favor or oppose such a plan? (December 1968)[a]		
Favor	29	73
Oppose	65	18
No opinion	6	9

[a] Respondents to this question were labelled as "whites" and "non-whites."
Source: *The Gallup Poll: Public Opinion 1935–71* (New York: Random House, 1972), vol. 3.

Which three of these national problems would you like to see the government devote most of its attention to in the next year or two? (April 1970)

Ranking by the general population:
    reducing the amount of crime
    reducing pollution of air and water
    improving public education
    helping people in poor areas
    conquering "killer" diseases
    improving housing, clearing slums
    reducing racial discrimination
    reducing unemployment
    improving highway safety
    beautifying America

Ranking by blacks:
    improving housing, clearing slums
    helping people in poor areas
    reducing racial discrimination
    improving public education
    reducing unemployment
    reducing pollution of air and water
    reducing amount of crime
    conquering "killer" diseases
    improving highway safety
    beautifying America

blacks see the riots coming from "people being treated badly."

Even while recognizing cultural differences between blacks and whites, we should guard against being carried away with the differences. Blacks and whites have come to share many traits over the course of three hundred years. A perceptive book by Donald J. Devine records this black-white sharing of political culture. On most dimensions that he measures (a series of issues grouped under his label of "liberal tradition values"), he finds a sharing by majorities of both black and white respondents. Liberal values include a common national identity, community trust, support for the Constitution, popular rule, legislative predominance, federalism, decentralized parties, individual freedom, expectations of equality, property rights, and freedom of religion.

Table 5.4. **Public Opinion Survey
with Regard to Government, in Detroit, by Race**

	Whites	*Blacks*
How much do you think you can trust the government in (Washington/Detroit) to do what is right: just about always, most of the time, some of the time, or almost never? (1971)		
Trust in the Washington government:		
About always or most of the time	57%	28%
Some of the time or almost never	43	72
Trust in the Detroit government:		
About always or most of the time	46	24
Some of the time or almost never	54	76
Some people say policemen lack respect or use insulting language. Others disagree. Do you think this happens in this neighborhood? (1971)		
Yes	11	36
No	81	58
Don't know	7	6
Some people say policemen search and frisk people without good reasons. Others disagree. Do you think this happens to people in this neighborhood? (1971)		
Yes	10	37
No	82	59
Don't know	8	5
Some people say policemen use unnecessary force in making arrests. Others disagree. Do you think this happens to people in this neighborhood? (1971)		
Yes	8	34
No	85	61
Don't know	7	6

Source: Joel D. Aberbach and Jack L. Walker, *Race in the City: Political Trust and Public Policy in the New Urban System* (Boston: Little, Brown, 1973), pp. 49, 52.

Table 5.5. Public Opinion Survey in Detroit with Respect to Civil Disorders, 1967, by Race

	Whites	Blacks
Which of the following comes closest to explaining why the [respondent's term for the event] took place: People were being treated badly, criminals did it, people wanted to take things?		
People being treated badly	28%	69%
Criminals did it	31	11
People wanted to take things	37	18
Other	2	4
Do you think most of the Negro community supported the [respondent's term for the event], or about half did, or just a few did?		
Most	6	6
About half	25	12
Few	69	82
Do you sympathize with the people who took part in the [respondent's term for the event]: Yes, somewhat, no?		
Yes	9	30
Somewhat	9	16
No	82	54

Source: Joel D. Aberbach and Jack L. Walker, *Race in the City: Political Trust and Public Policy in the New Urban System* (Boston: Little, Brown, 1973), pp. 49, 52, 57.

An exception to Devine's discovery of common black and white support for national values lies in "community trust," where a substantial majority of blacks show a lack of trust.[6] With respect to their support of other values: blacks tend to give less support than whites; still, over 80 percent of blacks feel their country is worth fighting for, 60 percent feel that Congress was helpful to their rights, and 65 percent feel the Supreme Court has been helpful.[7]

6. Donald J. Devine, *The Political Culture of the United States: The Influence of Member Values on Regime Maintenance* (Boston: Little, Brown, 1973), pp. 270–80.
7. Ibid., pp. 279–80.

We should also guard against the mistaken effort to measure the presence of two nations in this country by reference to *black* attitudes alone. White prejudice has at least something to do with distinctive black attitudes, and white prejudice is still with us. We can see some positive changes in white attitudes toward blacks in the information provided by table 5.6. Americans are now substantially more willing to say that blacks are as intelligent as whites, and that they would vote for a black presidential candidate nominated by their party. Yet there seems to be a greater willingness to express non-prejudiced sentiments in the abstract than when they are tied to a tangible event in one's own situation. Table 5.7 is taken from Devine's discussion of tradition values put under stress. In each instance, he shows that respondents become *more* prejudiced as they perceive an actual encounter with blacks.

Table 5.6. **Changes in White Attitudes Toward Blacks**

Political equality for blacks:

QUESTION: If your party nominated a generally well qualified man for president, and he happened to be a Negro, would you vote for him?

	1958	1963	1965	1967	1969
Yes	38%	47%	59%	54%	67%
No	53	45	34	40	23
No opinion	9	8	7	6	10

Perceptions of black intelligence:

	1942	1944	1946	1968
Negroes as intelligent	42%	44%	53%	58%
Not as intelligent	48	48	40	14
Don't know	10	8	7	28

Source: Donald J. Devine, *The Political Culture of the United States: The Influence of Member Values on Regime Maintenance* (Boston: Little, Brown, 1973), pp. 335, 337.

Table 5.7. **The Effect of Prejudice Stimuli upon Tradition Values**

Tradition Value Support	Value under Stress	Loss of Support from Stress
1. Everyone in America should have equal opportunities to get ahead.	1. I would be willing to have a Negro as my supervisor in my place of work.	
Agree 98%	Agree 60%	38%
Undecided 0	Undecided 2	
Disagree 2	Disagree 38	
2. All people should be treated as equals in the eyes of the law.	2. If I went on trial I would not mind having Negroes on the jury.	
Agree 98	Agree 76	22
Undecided 0	Undecided 5	
Disagree 2	Disagree 19	
3. People should help each other in time of need.	3. If a Negro's home burned down, I would be willing to take his family into my home for a night.	
Agree 99	Agree 64	35
Undecided 1	Undecided 6	
Disagree 0	Disagree 30	
4. Children should have equal educational opportunities.	4. I would not mind having Negro children attend the same school my children go to.	
Agree 98	Agree 79	19
Undecided 1	Undecided 2	
Disagree 1	Disagree 19	

Table 5.7. (continued)

Tradition Value Support	Value under Stress	Loss of Support from Stress
5. Everyone should have equal right to hold public office. Agree 91 Undecided 1 Disagree 8	5. I believe that I would be willing to have a Negro represent me in the Congress of the U.S. Agree 71 Undecided 6 Disagree 23	20
6. Each person should be judged according to his own individual worth. Agree 97 Undecided 1 Disagree 2	6. I would not mind if my children were taught by a Negro schoolteacher. Agree 67 Undecided 8 Disagree 35	30
7. I believe in the principle of brotherhood among men. Agree 94 Undecided 5 Disagree 1	7. I would be willing to invite Negroes to a dinner party in my home. Agree 29 Undecided 4 Disagree 67	65
8. Public facilities should be equally available to everyone. Agree 83 Undecided 4 Disagree 14	8. I would be willing to stay at a hotel that accommodated Negroes as well as whites. Agree 61 Undecided 4 Disagree 35	22

Table 5.7. (continued)

Tradition Value Support	Value under Stress	Loss of Support from Stress
9. Under our democratic system people should be allowed to live where they please if they can afford it.	9. I would be willing to have a Negro family live next door to me.	
Agree 60	Agree 35	25
Undecided 6	Undecided 2	
Disagree 34	Disagree 63	
10. I believe that all public recreational facilities should be available to all people at all times.	10. I don't think I would mind if Negro children were to swim in the same pool as my children.	
Agree 63	Agree 38	25
Undecided 6	Undecided 8	
Disagree 31	Disagree 54	

Source: Frank R. Westie, "The American Dilemma: An Empirical Test," *American Sociological Review* (August 1965): 531–32, as presented in Donald J. Devine, *The Political Culture of the United States: The Influence of Member Values on Regime Maintenance* (Boston: Little, Brown, 1973), pp. 341–42.

Black Economy

In erecting the image of a black nation within the United States, it is not enough to document the distinctive attitudes of blacks and whites. There is also a distinctive *economy* in the black nation. This goes beyond the obvious finding that blacks are poorer than whites, with jobs more often at the lower ends of the income and status hierarchies. Urban economists have described several features of the black ghetto that produce continued economic subordination to the white nation. As described by Frank G. Davis:[8]

1. A differential of 13 to 19 percent between the wages of whites and nonwhites remains even after adjusting for white-nonwhite differences in education, age, region, and size of city. This differential reflects discrimination or the structural elements that develop in the ghetto economy.

2. There is a net *outflow* of capital resources from the ghetto. This reflects purchases made by black businesses (mainly small retail and food shops) from outside the ghetto, imports of goods and exports of profits by white-owned businesses, and the export of black labor to employers outside the ghetto.

3. The high concentration of low-income residences in the ghetto attracts small-scale, low-profit retail activities. Due to land scarcity and high land values, there are few high-profit manufacturing activities in the ghetto.

4. Black-owned businesses in the ghetto tend to be smaller and financially more precarious than the "white-enclave" businesses, thus minimizing any hopes for a burgeoning of black capitalism.

5. High-wage industries locate in the low land-value suburban areas, imposing transportation costs on black laborers that make the wages for unskilled labor uneconomic for ghetto blacks. "The result is the simultaneous existence of job vacancies and unemployed black labor." [9]

8. This section relies heavily on Frank G. Davis, *The Economics of Black Community Development: Analysis and Program for Autonomous Community Development* (Chicago: Markham, 1972).

9. Ibid., p. 104.

Some traits of the larger economy also have consequences for the ghetto:

1. Industrial investments promote technological changes that reduce the need for unskilled labor.
2. Black laborers are forced to compete among themselves for jobs in low-productivity, low-paying service industries where blacks are already concentrated. As inflation boosts the prices that blacks must pay for consumer goods, there is likely to be further lag in the incomes of unskilled workers.

Davis is pessimistic about the promise of black capitalism for the ghetto. In his view, the structure of black enterprise will not generate a large volume of business or high rates of employment. There remains the problem of residential land values that prohibit large-scale industrialization in the ghetto. Manpower training programs have not reached the mass of unemployed blacks: over a six-year period, on-the-job trainees included only 1.4 percent the estimated number of black unemployed.

Some programs may increase the number or the wealth of black entrepreneurs but leave untouched the major forces producing black poverty. "Mere substitution of black capitalists for white capitalists under present conditions of resource use is far from an optimum economic condition of ghetto development and growth and could have only minimal effects." [10] Davis urges community ownership of ghetto resources. He would have the sectors of manufacturing and distribution controlled by the community, with the retention of profits as well as labor wages in the community. Davis' analysis is provocative, but it does not reckon with the likely opposition

10. Ibid., p. 114.

from aspiring black capitalists, as well as from white politicians who would be asked to authorize grants of capital and the regulatory actions needed to establish such ventures.[11]

Black Government

Along with the distinctive culture and economy, there is also government in the black nation. *Quasi-government* is probably a more accurate term, insofar as key components are voluntary institutions whose leaders interact and set the tones that become the "judgments" of the black community. While no legal authority attaches to many of these leaders, they "assemble and utilize various combinations of the fundamental political resources: money, office, prestige, technical knowledge, the capacity for eliciting a mass response, or the capacity for utilizing physical force." [12] Leaders come to their positions through prominent organizations: large churches, CORE (Congress of Racial Equality), NAACP (National Association for the Advancement of Colored People), the Panthers, or through election to a prominent public office. Black mayors of large cities and members of the United States Senate and House of Representatives are important leaders in the black nation. Because this leadership is only quasi-governmental, there is some fluidity in its composition and no little disagreement as to the pecking order among leaders. A 1968 survey is useful in showing the diversity in the black leadership, even if it cannot provide a current list of the top figures. Black respondents gave at least 10 percent of their nominations to four persons defined as "a leader to whom you would give active support": Ralph Abernathy, Roy Wilkins, Carl Stokes, and Whitney Young. Three other figures received

11. See also Carolyn Shaw Bell, *The Economics of the Ghetto* (New York: Norton, 1972).

12. Holden, *Politics of the Black Nation*, pp. 4–5.

the nomination of at least 15 percent of black respondents as "people you disagree with most": Stokely Carmichael, H. Rap Brown, and Elijah Muhammed. There is further commentary on differences in black and white politics in that Senator Edward Brooke of Massachusetts was about the most acceptable black leader to white respondents, but one of the least acceptable to blacks.[13]

Among the problems of black leaders are some traits in their own culture. Holden finds black leaders constantly subject to cynicism and distrust, with many blacks inclined to see any successful leader as becoming a "Tom" and selling out his people for the perquisites of his office.[14]

What kinds of strategies do the black leaders pursue? Here again we can see themes of the black culture. Holden identifies the strategies of clientage, opposition, and withdrawal. Each rests on the assumption that there are black and white nations with different interests, and with the resources disproportionately located in the white nation. *Clientage* seeks benefits through alliances with white leaders: "If you haven't got power yourself, keep powerful friends." [15] Clientage can include a variety of tactics, ranging from subservience (Tomming) to the organization of a protest demonstration that might—perhaps by provoking an overreaction by white police officers—arouse support from potential white allies.[16]

Opposition, like clientage, assumes necessary linkages between blacks and whites, but opposition seeks to use constitutional procedure or moral suasion to bring about changes. It is a strategy of court battles, the pursuit of legislative enactments, and the dogging of administrators for proper rulings and enactments. It may coexist with clientage

13. Robert Chandler, *Public Opinion: Changing Attitudes in Contemporary Political and Social Issues* (New York: Bowker, 1972), p. 26.
14. Holden, *Politics of the Black Nation,* p. 145.
15. Ibid., p. 43.
16. See Michael Lipsky, *Protest in City Politics: Rent Strikes, Housing, and the Power of the Poor* (Chicago: Rand McNally, 1970).

on particular issues; but it is a more assertive strategy, less passive than clientage.[17]

Withdrawal differs from both clientage and opposition in questioning the interdependence of black and white nations. In its most pure form, withdrawal appears in demands for separate territory (e.g., black "states" within the United States), community-owned economic enterprises, community control over privately owned businesses in the ghetto, and assertions of violence as proper means for enforcing decisions of the black community.[18] Other tactics have some elements of withdrawal, but not to the extent that they would deny some points of integration with the larger polity. Limited demands for neighborhood control and the pursuit of guaranteed places for blacks in local, state, or national politics are examples. In these cases, there is no demand for complete separation or community control, but there is an assertion of the distinctiveness of the black community, plus demands for official black representations in larger arenas or for control over certain aspects of local public services.

In recent years the black nation has made real progress in the political sphere. From 1960 to 1971 the percentage of the black electorate registered to vote in the eleven states of the former Confederacy increased from 29.1 to 58.6. Black candidates are also winning an increasing number of contests in both South and North. In the period from 1970 to 1973, the number of elected black officeholders increased by 78 percent: from 1,472 to 2,621.[19] An optimistic perspective on these figures sees more successful black leaders having a joint stake in the satisfaction of their constituents' demands and in the vitality of the larger political system. As moderate black and white politicians (including, perhaps, George Wallace in

17. Holden, *Politics of the Black Nation,* pp. 43–69.
18. Ibid., pp. 70–85.
19. *Statistical Abstract of the United States, 1973* (Washington, D.C.: U.S. Government Printing Office, 1974), p. 378.

recent years) seek to build their careers by appealing across racial lines, the political system can remain viable while members of the black nation come to receive a greater share of its rewards.

Proposals for Governmental Change

The demand for community control is one of the most widely heard from black political leaders and intellectuals. It is not a simple issue that brings ready agreement, however. Disagreements grow out of the problem of limited resources within the black community, the reluctance of white politicians in control of larger jurisdictions to bankroll black community governments, and a host of particular questions concerning which kinds of public service lend themselves to community control and which should be the targets of black demands for control.

Matthew Holden takes a limited view of community control. He cautions that "a group is not, by virtue of being a 'community' group, either more representative or more competent." Further, as blacks come to control the governments of the city per se, they have more to lose than to gain by dismantling the centralized city structures. Holden also sees a size constraint: "As soon as one gets beyond the *big* cities (more than 500,000) one starts to encounter situations where community control makes no sense because the units will simply be too small." [20]

Ernest Patterson, a professor of political science and an administrator at the University of Colorado, takes a more expansive view of community control. For him, it is both more necessary and a more inclusive target than it is for Holden. Patterson calls it "natural-neighborhood government," finds it

20. Holden, *Politics of the Black Nation,* p. 148.

appropriate for each of the 89 cities over 50,000 population in which blacks comprise a sizable (20 percent) segment of the population.[21] He sees violence resulting if acceptable modes of decentralization do not come as a result of black demands. For Patterson, the present elitist-controlled system keeps blacks from being able to live as free humans.[22] Much of the problem, as he sees it, lies in established ways of structuring city government and choosing city employees:

> . . . it is now clear that neither the democratic ideology of equality of opportunity nor good government notions concerning "public-regarding" motivations are automatically served by civil service and/or merit. Indeed . . . civil service and/or merit help secure bureaucratic autonomy, shield patterns of institutional racism, and help exclude underrepresented blacks from the bureaucracy.[23]

Going beyond community control, other proposals for building black leverage into the institutions of American government include an ambitious restructuring of the federal system. Matthew Holden would amend the Constitution to provide statehood for each city with more than 500,000 population. This would add twenty-six new states. Holden is a careful analyst, and he is not sanguine about the prospects of his reform. Yet he feels that it would offer several advantages to the black nation.

Most obviously, Holden's proposal would facilitate black control of state governments. Fifteen of these large cities already have black populations in excess of 20 percent. Given the prominence of states in the structure of the national

21. Ernest Patterson, *Black City Politics* (New York: Dodd, Mead, 1974), p. 253.
22. Ibid., p. 296.
23. Ibid., pp. 4–5.

government (crucial in selecting presidential nominees in party primaries and conventions, and in gaining seats in the United States House and Senate), the proposal should also produce more federal aid for the problems of urban blacks. And insofar as city and state government boundaries would be identical, there would no longer be a siphoning-off of urban economic resources by state governments to meet the demands of rural populations.[24]

Holden also wants black access to the pinnacle of American power. In one essay, he urges concerted efforts to gain a place for a black among the President's central advisory group, as opposed to what has already been accomplished, i.e., token blacks somewhere in the lower echelons of the White House staff.[25] Elsewhere he proposes a constitutional amendment to expand the Presidency via the addition of several vice-presidents, with a "guarantee that at least one of these would be a black man." [26] This is not a simple idea that Holden suggests in isolation from other concerns. It fits into his proposals for enlarging the perspective of black leaders beyond the cities that currently provide their bases of support. The black vice-president would—in the natural course of politics—come out of these urban communities and would acquire a strategic position in domestic programming, seeing that black views were raised at the highest levels of government. The scheme for plural vice-presidents also fits Holden's view that the Presidency concentrates too many responsibilities for the intellectual, psychic, or physical capacities of any one man. His plural vice-presidency is a way to strengthen the Presidency and assumes some devolution of authorities within the group of President-plus-vice-presidents that would benefit the country as a whole as well as its black nation.[27]

24. Matthew Holden, Jr., *The White Man's Burden* (New York: Chandler, 1973), pp. 246–52.

25. Holden, *Politics of the Black Nation*, p. 205.

26. Holden, *White Man's Burden*, pp. 252–53.

27. Ibid.

Significance of the American Black Nation

The evidence for the existence of a "black nation" within the United States is substantial. It includes distinctive patterns in culture, public opinion, and economics; plus demands for formal control over local functions, and for greater access of black community leaders to positions of authority in state and national governments.

The Black Nation as a Poor Country
For the view that the United States should be seen as a developing country, this awareness of a black nation within it has several meanings. First, the black nation in the United States can be compared directly with the poor nations of Africa, Asia, and Latin America. Indeed, this is something that blacks themselves do. They draw parallels in terms of skin color, poverty relative to rich white nations, and economic exploitation. Recall the view of the ghetto economy as one that supplies unsophisticated goods (i.e., unskilled labor) to the larger economy; serves as a market for sophisticated goods manufactured in the outside economy; and is penetrated by (colonial) entrepreneurs who are, in fact, the most successful businessmen of the ghetto. This view of the black nation as a part of the Third World includes a feeling of particularly close identification with the newly independent countries of Africa and comes along with programs of African-language instruction in inner-city high schools and in black community organizations; ethnic history programs designed to create greater awareness of the American community's African roots; black tour groups chartering flights and hotel accommodations in Africa; plus political and financial support for the liberation movements in southern Africa.

There is a second parallel in policy priorities between American blacks and the poor countries that has particular relevance for the issue of economic growth as opposed to the conservation of natural resources. Both America's poor black nation and the poor nations of the world are less concerned with limiting economic growth and conserving the environment at the status quo than are their affluent white counterparts. American blacks and poor countries demonstrate a point that we shall make more directly in the following chapter: concerns with conservation are more a luxury of the well-to-do than a uniform preoccupation of mankind.

For the American black nation, this relative lack of concern with conserving the environment appears in the black press and in some public-opinion polls. Recall the data in table 5.3 showing the ordering by black and white respondents of the most important policy issues. For whites, "reducing pollution of air and water" was second in importance, right behind "reducing the amount of crime." For blacks, however, the pollution item was sixth in importance. Higher in their priorities were items that seem more oppressive to a ghetto resident: housing, poverty, racial discrimination, public education, and unemployment. A reading of editorials and letters in black newspapers suggests the same kind of ordering. Concern about air and water pollution, the preservation of wilderness areas, or the protection of wildlife does not receive the coverage found in the white press. Editorials and letters in the *Chicago Defender* during the spring of 1974, for example, emphasized school segregation, crime, housing, the promotion of black candidates for public office, black pride, the problems of blacks in local government bureaucracies, the cause of African liberation, plus a number of items found at that time in any paper having a heavily Democratic readership: inflation, unemployment, tax inequities, and the impeachment of Richard Nixon.

This is not to say that the black community has no concern with environmental issues. Nevertheless, its focus in this area is more specialized than that found in the white community.

During the spring of 1974, the *Chicago Defender* was narrowly concerned with industrial pollution that affects ghetto air. A dramatic case occurred in Chicago late in April 1974, when a southside industrial accident vented a large amount of noxious gas, caused a great deal of discomfort in the nearby ghetto, some hospitalizations, and the evacuation of residents. The event received major coverage in the local black press; it preempted the front page for several days and took sizable space in news columns, editorials, and letters to the editor.

For the poor countries of the world, a parallel set of priorities became evident at the United Nations Conference on the Human Environment, conducted at Stockholm during 1972. In formal papers and oral presentations, the representatives of poor countries emphasized their poverty and their inability to pay the costs of dealing with their environmental problems. They also focused on a set of problems more elementary than those in the richer countries: urban sewage and water, and the effluent of industrial plants subject to no pollution abatements whatsoever. There were some moments of acrimony in Stockholm when representatives of the poor nations accused their affluent counterparts of seeking to put a brake on economic growth just at the point where some progress seemed within the grasp of the poor. In their eyes, this was a new variant of neocolonialism: denying to the poor countries the same disregard for environmental conservation that helped the presently developed countries achieve their industrialization in the past. Representatives of poor countries see that rich countries can afford investments in growth despite payments made to protect their environments, and can export some costs of their environmental protection to the poor countries as part of the increased prices of manufactured goods.[28]

The case of Indian automobiles is instructive. These little cars (carrying four passengers at American standards of fit)

28. *Report of the United Nations Conference on the Human Environment: Stockholm, 5–16 June 1972* (New York: United Nations, 1973), pp. 45–48.

produce several times the air pollution of larger and more powerful American cars, even when the Indian vehicles are new and well tuned. As more of the Indian cars seem to be coughing down the highways and belching smoke, the actual differential in favor of American cars is probably far greater. The United States government now requires Americans to pay something like 10 percent of a car's initial cost in pollution-control devices. For the Indians to require that expenditure would be to price many potential vehicles off the road. Environmental cleanliness is a luxury currently beyond most Indians' ability, just as a preoccupation with the environment is outside the concerns of many American blacks.

Black-White Dualism as a Parallel to Poor-Country Dualism

A further significance of the black and white nations within the United States is the parallel to the ethnic and economic dualisms found in most poor countries. Just as our black nation is subordinate to the white majority in terms of economic resources, education, health, housing, protection from crime, and political power, so are most poor countries affected by internal contrasts between rich and poor regions, tribes, races, or castes. The most striking dualisms are those—like the case of American blacks and whites—where there is an overlay of economic, social, and political advantages and disadvantages: where the poor sector is also low status culturally and least powerful politically. The debates in those countries that have faced their dualisms are not unlike those in the United States that deal with black-white differentials: they focus on the responsibility of the central government for promoting economic growth and social advancement in the depressed sectors. Counter demands come from well-to-do interests who assert that investments should focus on those sectors having ready supplies of skilled personnel, where the investments will pay off with more speed and certainty. Also in the United

States and elsewhere, statements of caution came from those groups having political power and not wanting to see it diluted through a forced sharing of prized offices with those who are currently underrepresented.

Amelioration from American Affluence

Where the United States differs sharply from other developing countries that have a problem of dualism is in its economic capacity to do something about it. Here the aggregate levels of resources make it easier to provide more to the poor sectors. Evidence for this lies in the rates of economic and social progress for our black nation, as shown in table 5.8, and in the

Table 5.8. **White and Black Economic and Social Trends**

Median Family Income	1959	1971
White	$5,928	$10,622
Black	3,010	6,440
Black as percent of white	50.8	60.6

School Enrollment, 1960–72	White	Black and Other
Percent change		
High school	+42	+96
College	+123	+277

Percent of Population Completing	White	Black
High school, 1960	25.8	12.9
College, 1960	8.1	3.1
High school, 1972	36.4	24.9
College, 1972	12.6	5.1

Black as Percent of White Completing	1960	1972
High school	50.0	68.5
College	38.3	40.5

Source: Statistical Abstract of the United States, 1973 (Washington, D.C.: U.S. Government Printing Office, 1974), pp. 110, 115, 333.

material from chapter 2, showing that resources in the United States are distributed more evenly than is the case in the very poor countries.

As we noted in the discussion of urban problems, however, the amelioration of blacks' material needs does not eliminate the tensions between rich and poor. If black aspirations are like the rabbit at the dog track—as seen by Edward Banfield—they will keep ahead of progress and render it insufficient. Many differences between blacks and whites that justify the concept of two nations are not economic in nature. They reflect different histories and attitudes. These draw some of their strength from economic differentials, but they seem likely to survive whatever economic narrowing occurs in the next few years. Indeed, we should ask ourselves if we want all the noneconomic features of our distinct black and white nations to disappear. For those who value differences in culture and politics for their own sake—because they help make life more exciting and may provide a backdrop of tolerance for other groups whose life styles or political views differ from the majority—the distinctiveness of the black nation is one of the bright spots in the United States. Even while some of its economic and social problems lessen the life chances of individual blacks, other features of the black nation deserve applause. Among the many kinds of ethnic, cultural, and political heterogeneity that exist in the United States, that of the black community may be the most important in its distinctiveness and in the number of people involved, and it may be a positive force in strengthening the tolerance that benefits other people who are distinctive, but not black.

6

☆

ECONOMIC GROWTH: THREAT TO SOCIETY OR ENGINE OF SOCIAL PROGRESS?

It is wise at this point to sum up the main argument and to ask where it is taking us. Previous chapters have claimed that the United States resembles the poor countries of the world on certain traits, especially in its dualisms, or contrasting economic, social, and political conditions between wealthier and poorer sectors of the population. The United States does not score as high on worldwide comparisons that measure the quality of life (e.g., education, housing, health care) or the equal distribution of benefits as it does on measures of sheer economic wealth. Signs of lagged development show up clearly in comparisons of more-developed and less-developed states and regions; depressed central cities and affluent suburbs; and white and black racial groups.

With all these indications of social and economic sectors still having an interest in rapid development, however, the United States also shows signs of advanced—some would say excessive—development. This country is fabulously wealthy at the same time that it shows marked contrasts between comfort and poverty. The wealth has two implications for our analysis.

131

First, it presents the wherewithal to assist the economic needs of the less-developed sectors. Second, and more troubling, it generates sentiments that further economic growth offers more threat than promise; that the United States is already too developed and that further growth threatens fragile balances in natural and human situations.

This chapter focuses on the issue of development in the United States. It examines the arguments of those who feel that "enough is enough," and who have captured the attention of the "conventional wisdom" with their reasoning—at least insofar as the conventional wisdom is expressed by literate and liberal intellectuals. There are serious weaknesses in this antigrowth perspective; some of them are made clear by a counter perspective that has begun to be heard, and some appear in the earlier chapters of this book. Yet the pursuit of economic growth is not a simple task, and is not without its dangers for economic, social, and political issues of some importance. This chapter not only criticizes a simplistic "antigrowth" perspective on the future of the United States, but also considers some of the major problems as well as the benefits that are offered by the pursuit of growth. In seeking to chart the near future, it is guided by economists' studies of growth in the less-developed countries and by the recent experiences of the poor but developing states of the United States.

The Muddled Argument of Overdevelopment

The argument that the United States is overdeveloped is a simplified amalgam of several views. Numerous writers have expressed these views, but they do not share all features of the view to be outlined. Yet their work is sufficiently alike in its attachment to notions of dramatic economic and social changes in the recent history of the United States, and in its concern to control further growth, that it warrants this com-

mon treatment. By examining the work of several widely
hailed individuals who represent different strains in this literature, we can find important challenges for any theme that
supports continued economic growth. There are three principal thrusts in the view of the United States as overdeveloped.

1. The United States has moved into a new age. Daniel
Bell began a movement among intellectuals when he described
"postindustrial society." By this he meant the replacement of
manufacturing with service activities as the dominant feature
of the economy; the predominance of theoretical knowledge as
basic to the new economic order, with universities the institutions at the leading edge of continued change; and the importance of research and development activities, with government
increasing its role in the economy by funding R & D projects
that are beyond the resources of the private sector, and by
controlling the new technologies.[1]

2. The process of social and economic change has speeded
up to an unsettling degree, with society becoming hyper-
innovative. Alvin Toffler's *Future Shock* has gone through
some four editions and thirty-four printings attracting countless people to the argument that a triumvirate of *transcience,
novelty,* and *diversity* are the traits of today and tomorrow that
will produce the symptoms of social pathology. Writing with a
compelling force, he calls our society "super-industrial."

> Millions sense the pathology that pervades the air, but
> fail to understand its roots. These roots . . . are traceable
> . . . to the uncontrolled, non-selective nature of our lunge
> into the future. They lie in our failure to direct,
> consciously and imaginatively, the advance toward
> super-industrialism . . . the United States is a nation in
> which tens of thousands of young people flee reality by
> opting for drug-induced stupor or alcoholic haze; a

1. *The Coming of Post-Industrial Society* (New York: Basic, 1973).

nation in which legions of elderly folk vegetate and die
in loneliness; in which the flight from family and
occupational responsibility has become an exodus; in
which masses tame their raging anxieties with Miltown,
or Librium, or Equanil, or a score of other tranquilizers
and psychic pacifiers. Such a nation, whether it knows it
or not, is suffering from future shock.[2]

3. Growth not only has psychic costs, but also poses severe
physical threats. There are too many people, too much industrial production, and consumption of too many nonrenewable
resources. The result of all this glut is said to be impending
pollution that will stifle the environment. Paul Ehrlich, an
articulate professor of biology, looked ahead only ten years
from 1969 and saw an "eco-catastrophe."

The end of the ocean came late in the summer of 1979,
and it came even more rapidly than the biologists had
expected. There had been signs for more than a decade,
commencing with the discovery in 1968 that DDT slows
down photosynthesis in marine plant life. . . .
Other changes had taken place in 1975. Most ocean
fishes that returned to fresh water to breed, like the
salmon, had become extinct, their breeding streams so
dammed up and polluted that their powerful homing
instinct only resulted in suicide.[3]

In a more temperate and persuasive piece, a group of
researchers from the Massachusetts Institute of Technology
projected growth rates for population, industrial and food
production, resource consumption, and pollution. Their book,

2. Alvin Toffler, *Future Shock* (New York: Bantam, 1971), p. 366.
3. Paul Ehrlich, "Eco-Catastrophe," *Ramparts* (September 1969), as reprinted in Franklin Tugwell, ed., *Search for Alternatives: Public Policy and the Study of
the Future* (Cambridge, Mass.: Winthrop Publishers, 1973), especially p. 186.

The Limits to Growth, reports computer printouts showing "the basic behavior mode of the world system is exponential growth of population and capital, followed by collapse." [4] They note that "feedback loops" exist to perceive and react to excessive growth by control mechanisms, but find these feedback loops too slow for the rates of growth envisioned. The example of the Green Revolution (the introduction of new seed varieties combined with fertilizers and pesticides) shows how a seemingly attractive technological solution to the world's food shortages produced negative consequences not foreseen and uncontrolled because the innovations were introduced and disseminated too rapidly:

> Where ... conditions of economic inequality already
> exist, the Green Revolution tends to cause widening
> inequality. Large farmers generally adopt the new
> methods first. They have the capital to do so and can
> afford to take the risk. Although the new seed varieties
> do not require tractor mechanization, they provide much
> economic incentive for mechanization, especially where
> multiple cropping requires a quick harvest and
> replanting. On large farms, simple economic
> considerations lead almost inevitably to the use of
> labor-displacing machinery and to the purchase of still
> more land. The ultimate effects of this socio-economic
> positive feedback loop are agricultural unemployment,
> increased migration to the city, and perhaps even
> increased malnutrition, since the poor and unemployed
> do not have the means to buy the newly planted food.[5]

The Limits to Growth has been widely read and absorbed into the conventional wisdom of numerous countries. Over one

4. Donella H. Meadows et al., *The Limits to Growth* (New York: Universe, 1972), p. 142.
5. Ibid., p. 147.

million copies in some twenty languages have been sold. The publisher's blurb on the back cover of the American paperback edition gives some indication of its basic message and reception:

> The earth's interlocking resources—the global system of nature in which we all live—probably cannot support present rates of economic and population growth much beyond the year 2100, if that long, even with advanced technology.

And in the words of one well-known reader: "If this book doesn't blow everybody's mind who can read without moving his lips, then the earth is kaput."

Some Problems of an Overdeveloped United States

The view that growth produces doom makes serious demands on our attention. We cannot end this book with a simple recommendation to pursue growth without regard for avoidable consequences to the environment. Neither can we prescribe growth without regard for modes of distribution that will maximize the contribution that growth can make toward the amelioration of our social problems. Yet the simple assertion that growth produces doom is no better a place to end! Serious problems are inherent in that view. Not the least is its proponents' desire to have the benefits of a more equal distribution of benefits without permitting continued growth. In the words of the MIT volume:

> We unequivocally support the contention that a brake imposed on world demographic and economic growth spirals must not lead to a freezing of the *status quo* of economic development of the world's nations.

If such a proposal were advanced by the rich nations, it would be taken as a final act of neocolonialism. The achievement of a harmonious state of global economic, social, and ecological equilibrium must be a joint venture based on joint conviction, with benefits for all.[6]

What the MIT group lacks is a convincing demonstration that a strategy of *no* (or limited) growth will facilitate the redistribution of resources from rich to poor sectors. The group is putting its chips on the side of changes in values:

We affirm finally that any deliberate attempt to reach a rational and enduring state of equilibrium by planned measures, rather than by chance or catastrophe, must ultimately be founded on a basic change of values and goals at individual, national, and world levels.[7]

Such changes may occur, but it seems wiser to count on a projection of present values and figure out a way to inter- and intranational redistributions without waiting for utopia.

It is curious that the MIT group assumes a *stability* of present technology in its computer projections of economic growth, resource depletion, and pollution; but it then abandons this assumption of stability with respect to political values when offering policy recommendations. There is an appealing counter argument that assumes a stability of political values: a more equal distribution of opportunities and resources should occur via low-cost education and training, health services, transfer payments and other welfare programs in a more affluent and continuously growing economy where the well-

6. Ibid., p. 194; this language is not that of the research team per se, but is a commentary by the Club of Rome, i.e., the sponsor of the MIT group's research.

7. Meadows et al., *Limits to Growth*, p. 195; this also is the language of the Club of Rome.

to-do can tolerate greater levels of taxation without feeling significant loss of their *own* opportunities.

There have been serious efforts at challenging the growth-produces-doom perspective with fresh information and reanalyses of the data used by the MIT group. The thrust of this work is threefold: (1) growth is not so rapid or universal as viewed by the doomsters, and does not so clearly threaten resource depletion or stifling pollution; (2) projections of unlimited growth have not reckoned with the continued growth of technologies that could blunt the adverse consequences; and (3) the issue of growth vs. no-growth is a sterile debate that distracts attention from the more important concerns of "what kind of growth?" and "how should its output be distributed?"

One group of demographers has challenged any projections that see population as going continuously upward. Their argument has two basic points. First, that population forecasting should *not* be accepted without strong reservations:

No demographer has ever succeeded in forecasting the future of any population. However, demographers today are much better informed about the reasons for their failure, and their product is much more likely to be regarded with justifiable doubt. We call that progress.[8]

Second, figures that do exist about recent trends severely question any expectation of continued population growth. Indeed, the long-term trend among countries with advanced levels of economic development is population *decline.* This is also true of the United States, with the magnitude and duration of our post-World War II "baby boom" being not the typical but the aberrant phenomenon. That boom seems to

8. Norman B. Ryder, "The Future Growth of the American Population," in Charles F. Westoff et al., *Toward the End of Growth: Population in America* (Englewood Cliffs, N.J.: Prentice-Hall, 1973), pp. 85–86.

have passed in the mid-1960s, with the mean birth ratio declining by some 20–24 percent between 1961–65 and 1966–70.[9] Declines have come partly with changes in technology (more widespread use of better contraception) and values (later marriages and fewer children wanted). While this group of researchers did not extend their analyses beyond countries with "developed" economies, the implication of their work is that economic growth brings a modernization of attitudes and life styles, and fewer children. Occasional upward spurts in population occur, but there seems little in recent history to support any notions of continued exponential growth.

A group of researchers from Sussex University in England takes direct aim at the MIT group. Their volume is titled *Models of Doom: A Critique of the Limits to Growth* and offers a systematic attack on the assumptions, methods, conclusions, and recommendations offered by their New England colleagues.[10] This is not the place to referee the international match and award a cup to the winning university, but we can array the Sussex counterargument against the growth-produces-doom perspective. The Sussex group finds the MIT people to be unreconstructed Malthusians, likely to err for the same reasons as their predecessor. The essence of Malthus' forecast was that population would grow exponentially, while food production would grow only arithmetically. Malthus offered predictions from the early nineteenth century that, if true, would have had most of us starving long before now.

The Sussex group challenges their colleagues for the failure to build changes in technology into their computer projections. They remind us that Malthus was proved wrong on the basis of higher agricultural yields as well as on the uneven nature of population growth. Moreover, the process of

9. Norman B. Ryder, "Recent Trends and Group Differences in Fertility," in ibid., pp. 66–67.

10. H. S. D. Cole et al., *Models of Doom: A Critique of the Limits to Growth* (New York: Universe, 1973).

technological innovation has continued throughout the period since Malthus. If we accept Toffler's view, technological innovation may be the most rapid of the many contemporary changes. Just as any forecasting of energy supplies done in the mid-nineteenth century could not have taken into consideration the as yet undeveloped use of petroleum, so any energy projections to the year 2100 must concede some unexpected progress toward discovery and innovation.

Sussex also indicts MIT for working with a whole-world model and thereby masking the numerous opportunities for continued resource exploitation, industrialization, and population growth in as yet undeveloped regions. One quotation from the Sussex report brings together several strands of its critique:

> In the early 19th century, Malthus predicted that all the world's arable land would soon be used up—including that in the Americas. According to data presented in the Technical Report [of the MIT group], less than 50 per cent of the world's potentially arable land is at present under cultivation. In the densely populated continents of Europe and SE Asia, the percentage is over 80; in North America and the USSR it is between 50 and 60; and in Africa, Australasia and South America it is around 15 to 20. In North America, Australasia and Argentina, land yields are low by world standards but the degree of mechanization is high, thereby suggesting that in these regions of the world the relatively scarce factor in agriculture is labour, not land. Indeed in some of these regions, arable land is being taken out of use.[11]

A group of students at Stanford have also published a

11. Ibid., p. 59.

critique of *Limits to Growth* and offer some projections of their own. They charge that "the MIT models appear to have started with a conclusion, limits to growth, and worked backward ... in such a manner as to force the conclusion." The Stanford group also endorses the Sussex claim that the MIT models are too static. "The models are not sensitive to feedback between the system's performance and the behavioral aspects, such as sociocultural changes leading to priority shifts and behavioral modification." [12]

The Sussex group concedes there are theoretical limits to growth, but it is more impressed with the political than the physical constraints. The 1973–74 oil embargo and price hike are recent cases in point. By admitting some degree of technological change into their models, Sussex pushes the point of resource depletion beyond the time span of its computer projections. For Sussex, the issue is not growth vs. no-growth, but the *nature* of growth, its *location,* and the *use* of its outputs. These issues lend themselves to political analysis, which must focus on the most variable of elements that do not lend themselves to computer projection.

> Some types of growth are quite consistent not merely with conservation of the environment, but with its enhancement. The problem in our view, is a socio-political one of stimulating this type of growth and of more equitable distribution, both between countries and within them.[13]

The Sussex group questions the social goals of the MIT researchers. It finds the New Englanders loyal to the intellec-

12. Marc U. Porat and Wesley Martin, eds., "World IV: A Policy Simulation Model of National and Regional Systems," *Stanford Journal of International Studies* 9 (Spring 1974): 71–166.

13. Cole, *Models of Doom,* p. 10.

tual and leisure values of their class. There is in the MIT perspective "an aristocratic concern for enjoying amenity and environment without disturbance by others." [14] The MIT group excludes from the no-growth prescription—and, indeed, welcomes the further development of—those virtues "that many people would list as the most desirable and satisfying activities of man—education, art, music, religion, basic scientific research, athletics, and social interactions." [15] This may be the list of "most desirable" items named by "many people," but such judges would likely enunciate their preferences with the accents of the well-educated upper classes. Sussex doubts that the MIT group can acquire more tangible values (such as a more equal distribution of incomes) without economic growth.

The work of the Sussex and Stanford groups are sophisticated challenges to *The Limits to Growth*. Other challenges to the limited-growth perspective are appearing in the popular literature. One example is a book whose title makes very clear its message: *The DDT Myth: Triumph of the Amateurs* by Rita Gray Beatty.[16] According to the author, large numbers of citizens and government officials have been sold a misleading tale about DDT. The pesticide has been banned from widespread use, and people—especially people in low-income countries—face disease and hunger as a result. Ms. Beatty's argument is relevant to ours. DDT is a cheap ingredient of economic growth that promises to increase agricultural yields and keep people healthy. Its attackers ban its use because of its alleged harm to birds, animals, and man. The ban on DDT is, indeed, one of the more popular rallying cries of people who share the antigrowth perspective. According to Rita Beatty and the authorities she cites, the anti-DDT campaign has been marked by a partial and distorted reading of the scientific evidence, a failure to consider the costs in financial and human

14. Ibid., p. 148.
15. Ibid., p. 175.
16. New York: John Day, 1973.

terms of banning DDT, and no little self-serving on the part of the chemical's opponents. She cites evidence to counter the claims of those who view DDT as reducing the populations of songbirds and other species, and as being a health threat to humans. She also relates episodes of agricultural and health disasters coming with the end of DDT's use.

Another entry in this literature, "Against the Neo-Malthusians," appeared in *Commentary*.[17] Contrary to the dire predictions of *Limits to Growth,* B. Bruce Briggs cites the calculations of the Hudson Institute showing it possible for there to be

> a world of 15–20 billion people with an average per capita income of $20,000 (the current figures are just under 4 billion and $1,200; per capita income in the U.S. is $6,000). . . . Such a world could afford to pay for low-quality resources, massive pollution control, and plenty more, while leaving more than enough personal consumption income equivalent to that of an upper-middle-class American today. What is striking about the Hudson world is that it would function with present known and proven technology; no innovations would be necessary to make it work—no solar, geothermal, or fusion power, no artificial food, no cheap space travel.

What can a layman do with this muddle of contradictory claims, each citing scientific authority? One temptation is to attribute a selfish or ideological stance to one's protagonist. Briggs joins the Sussex group in suggesting that the limits-to-growth perspective has particular appeal to those among the affluent who do not want to share the goodies:

17. B. Bruce Briggs, "Against the Neo-Malthusians," *Commentary* 58 (July 1974): 25–29.

Mass prosperity has eroded the quality of life of the
upper-middle classes. When Yellowstone Park was
established a century ago for the benefit of all, only a few
could spare the time and money to visit it. Now that
every second factory worker has a camper, one must wait
in line to view Old Faithful. Once upon a time firearms
were too expensive to be bought casually, now the
discriminating duckhunter must share his blind with
Archie Bunker. . . . Impending prosperity throughout the
whole world is an even more frightening prospect.
Already the nouveaux bourgeois of Europe and Japan
have made themselves felt in this country as tourists and
investors. . . . Small wonder, then, that at the 1972
Stockholm Conference on the Environment the
industrial nations warned the less developed about the
evils of growth, and smaller wonder still that Third
World countries viewed the warning as another
neo-colonialist plot to keep them in their place.

Earlier chapters made the point that affluence accompanies a concern with environmental protection. The emphasis
on conservation or economic growth in the policies of American states follows cleavages in current levels of development.
The poorer states are more concerned with growth, and less
concerned with conservation. American blacks are more likely
to favor policies that will improve their standards of living,
while whites are more likely to support conservation of the
environment. Among countries of the world, the rich are more
willing to keep things as they are, while the poor demand
growth.

In the dispute about curtailing growth, we already hear
the active voices of those who suffer losses from stark conservation. Success in the campaigns to reduce population growth
has made problems for those industries and professions
dealing with babies and youngsters. A recent issue of *Business*

Week featured an article on the Gerber company, and its need to shift from a reliance on baby food.[18] An article in the *San Francisco Examiner* headlined *Too Many Doctors, Shortage of Babies* and commented on the untimely increase of pediatricians at an annual rate of 5 percent. According to the American Hospital Association, occupancy rates in pediatric hospital units are 40 percent and declining. The ratio of pediatricians to patients is one to 3,660 and is forecast as one to 1,869 by 1985.[19] There is a surplus of elementary school teachers across the country, and numerous communities have idled classrooms and whole school buildings erected within the past decade.

While there are no marked calls for more babies coming out of Gerber's, the medical professions, or the National Education Association, we may hear serious questioning about population levels as more occupational groups feel the pinch of stable and declining clientele. Studies of other countries have found public demands for more births, under stimuli such as declining economic growth, curtailed employment opportunities, needs for soldiers to defend against hostile neighbors, or reasons of national prestige. Bernard Berelson describes recent policies for birthrate increases in Japan, Israel, Argentina, France, Greece, Hungary, Bulgaria, Poland, and Rumania.

How can a country promote births? Berelson lists national payments for marriages and births, payments for delivery and confinement, guarantees of maternity leave with pay from the mother's employment, cash payments made to couples with large families, and tax concessions to the heads of large families.[20]

18. "The Lower Birth Rate Crimps the Baby Food Market," *Business Week*, 13 July 1974, pp. 44–50.

19. *San Francisco Examiner*, 24 October 1974, p. 34.

20. Bernard Berelson, "Population Growth Policy in Developed Countries," in Westoff et al., *End of Growth*, pp. 145–60.

The Club of Rome, a prestigious group of businessmen, scientists, and intellectuals that sponsored *The Limits to Growth,* has lent its name to a subsequent effort. According to a prepublication review, *Mankind at the Turning Point* makes some changes in the techniques of projection which provoked much professional criticism of *The Limits to Growth.*[21]

Mankind at the Turning Point does not rely on single aggregate projections for the whole world but makes predictions for each of several regions having peculiar social, economic, and resource characteristics. Like its predecessor, however, it foresees catastrophe in a continuation of present growth rates. In order to curb the danger while offering some promise to the poor, it prescribes less industrial growth in the rich countries in order to allow more in the poor countries. These sentiments have a noble appeal, but hardly seem appropriate to the "me first" Hobbesianism that so often prevails in international politics.

The Pursuit of Growth and Equality

If there is great confusion over the issue of limiting growth because of the depletion of physical resources and pollution, there is even more confusion surrounding another, related issue. This concerns the question, *Who gets the benefits?* While it is the underlying thesis of this book that we should recognize and respond to the demands for economic growth that come out of the depressed sectors of the American economy, numerous social scientists argue that the primary beneficiaries of economic growth are the well-to-do.

21. Mihajlo Mesarovic and Eduard Pestel, *Mankind at the Turning Point.* The prepublication review is "The Club of Rome: Act Two," *Time,* 2 October 1974, pp. 107–9.

Growth as a Threat to Equality

According to an argument that appears widely,[22] the middle- and upper-income groups in developing societies take most advantage of the opportunities presented by economic growth. Further, the lower-income classes usually pay a disproportionate share of the cost of growth—by being shut out of opportunities, and by suffering the greatest damage from inflation in the cost of necessities. The well-to-do have the capital and the training. When outsiders offer irrigation and other new agricultural techniques, or new industrial processes, local people with capital can invest in the opportunities and local people with training can fill the new, high-paying jobs. The rural poor are forced off the land to make way for mechanization and the consolidation of holdings; they drift to the cities and find it impossible to compete for jobs that demand literacy and a certain level of mechanical training, or—at higher levels—familiarity with modern techniques of commerce and management. As inflation bids up prices for food, clothing, and housing, the poor generally have no organizational strength to assure that wages keep up with the cost of living—assuming they have jobs. In most poor countries, no viable programs offer adult training or assurances of medical care, adequate housing, and minimum incomes.

The result of economic growth, claim some observers, is that the poor become even poorer. Sometimes they become poor only in relative terms, as their incomes do not increase as rapidly as those of people more able to take advantage of new opportunities. Sometimes the poor lose in absolute terms; a combination of being forced out of subsistence agriculture plus inflation in the cost of living leaves them with less purchasing power than they had prior to economic growth.

22. See, for example, James D. Cockcroft et al., *Dependence and Underdevelopment: Latin America's Political Economy* (Garden City, N.Y.: Anchor, 1972); and Irma Adelman and Cynthia Taft Morris, *Economic Growth and Social Equity in Developing Countries* (Stanford, Calif.: Stanford University Press, 1973).

This argument—that growth increases the plight of the poor—may be less applicable to low-income sectors of the United States than it is to the poor classes of Africa, Asia, and Latin America. In the United States much of the expulsion from the land of the poor farmer, ignorant in the ways of the city, has already occurred. Also, less of our population is so totally lacking in skills as to be unable to benefit from expansions in industry and commerce. And our poor are more likely to encounter viable programs of job training and income security. Yet, if the argument has substantial merit for the poor countries, it should be considered for whatever threat it poses to the lowest-income sectors of this country.

When the growth-increases-poverty argument is examined closely for the poor countries, it displays several weaknesses. It is muddied with inadequate data, contradictory results, a tendency to examine only the short-run results of economic growth, and in some cases of ideological blindness that hide from the writers the counterindications in their own data and prose.

A book by Irma Adelman and Cynthia Taft Morris entitled *Economic Growth and Social Equity in Developing Countries*[23] displays several of these problems. This is only one book in a vast literature on economic development, but it warrants careful attention. A closely related earlier book by Adelman and Morris received wide attention.[24] Their more recent work is bound to be influential, even though it displays several weaknesses typical of the argument that *growth produces inequality*.

One problem in the recent Adelman-Morris book is a tendency to exaggerate actual findings. To read the third par-

---

23. Adelman and Morris, *Economic Growth.*
24. Irma Adelman and Cynthia Taft Morris, *Society, Politics, and Economic Development* (Baltimore, Md.: Johns Hopkins University Press, 1967).

agraph in the preface, one would think that the syndrome of growth begetting poverty was clear in their findings:

> The results of our analyses came as a shock to us. Although we had believed economic growth to have unfavorable social, cultural, and ecological consequences, we had shared the prevailing view among economists that economic growth was economically beneficial to most nations. . . . Our results proved at variance with our preconceptions. In view of their unexpectedness, we undertook a variety of cross-checks during the two years before we sought their present publication. Case studies and other historical and contemporary evidence coming to our attention have been so overwhelmingly consistent with our findings that, despite major data deficiencies, we present them here with considerable confidence in their validity.[25]

Reading further into the book, it becomes increasingly a surprise that the authors did not take more seriously their own candid admissions of limitations. They concede shortcomings in their information, much of which takes the form of crude estimates. Moreover, the authors rely on data that come mostly from the period around 1960. This means they are limited to "cross sectional" analysis, i.e., comparing the standing of one country to another at a single point of time, and assuming that the traits of one country somewhat further along the road of economic development will become those of other countries just starting out in development. Not only does this preclude any consideration of the changes that take place within countries as they actually develop, but the period of time under consideration means that the authors are leaving out more

25. Adelman and Morris, *Economic Growth*, pp. vii–viii.

than a decade of the most recent experience. For almost all the African countries, the time frame limits their examination to the colonial period, when growth would presumably be of a kind to benefit primarily the more affluent European settlers and businessmen.

In interpreting their results, Adelman and Morris limit themselves to the short-run results from economic growth and concentrate mostly on the record of the poorest of the developing countries. Thus, they examine the points of change (actually simulated change, as noted above) closest to the early stages of growth, when economies would appear to be most vulnerable to the displacement of unsophisticated persons without adequate opportunities for the least trained of them. In colonial Africa, where very poor people were still outside the relevant political process, it should come as no surprise that their needs were given little consideration.

Growth as an Engine of Social Progress
To be candid with respect to the thesis of this book, there is not a great deal of evidence to show that the pursuit of economic development results in significant benefit for all income groups. Some evidence supports this expectation, however, if one is willing to accept a longer time perspective than that employed by Adelman and Morris. We have already seen that countries with the highest levels of economic development also have the most equal distributions of income, i.e., the countries of Northern and Western Europe, North America, Israel, Australia, and New Zealand.[26] This list includes the United States; and within the United States, states with the most affluent economies—like New Jersey, Connecticut, and

26. See the discussion on pages 24–26.

Ohio—tend to present the most equal distributions of income.[27]

It is not easy to determine how economic growth leads to more equality. There is much argument about this issue. One model that agrees with the data indicates an initial period of greater *inequality* during the growth process, followed by long-run changes in the direction of greater *equality*. The early negative change may occur as growth begins in the more so-phisticated industrial and urban sectors and provides im-mediate rewards for those workers who can meet the qualifications of training and skill. In many less-developed countries, growth produces a movement from rural to urban areas and a shift in employment opportunities from low wages to high wages that skews further the existing gaps between income brackets. An early emphasis on capital-intensive in-dustry is likely to put the premium on high-skill employment and thus skew distribution toward greater inequality. Nevertheless, a growing economy also expands employment opportunities at all levels; total employment may grow faster than the available work force, with increased opportunities appearing at all skill levels. As more low-skilled people move from unemployed to employed status, the distribution of in-comes moves in the direction of greater equality. With growth continuing, an economy should reach the position of the "developed economies," where generous programs of income transfers, low-cost or free education and health care can en-hance equalization opportunities across regional and genera-tional lines. During the period of growth, the timing and extent of early-inequality/later-equality may vary with such things as

27. Thomas R. Dye, "Income Inequality and American State Politics," *American Political Science Review* 63 (March 1969): 157–62. For the period covered by Dye's article, the coefficient of simple correlation between state-by-state Gini coefficients and median family income was -.77, indicating that high-income states generally have the more equal distributions of income.

the capital intensity of the first developments, and governmental efforts to speed or slow the rate of growth. Some studies of a Brazilian growth spurt beginning in the mid-1960s indicate early changes in the direction of greater *inequality;* but later shifts opened opportunities across the skill ranges, made jobs available to more workers, and produced a more equal distribution of incomes.[28]

Economic and Political Problems
Along the Route to Growth

An earlier chapter noted parallels between poor countries and poor American states, and suggested that some of these parallels—governmental centralization, political concentration, tax and spending regressivity—might contribute to economic development. As that chapter noted, the dynamics of economic growth are complex, and it is premature to cast these observations of parallels between the least-developed states and least-developed countries into a theory of development. The syndrome of centralization-concentration-regressivity may actually *impede* economic progress when government leaders use their positions to enhance their own prerogatives at public expense. Ghana, Uganda, and Indonesia provide examples of authoritarian leaders who used the advantages of centralization, political concentration, and regressive taxes to build uneconomic monuments, to support lavish life styles of their own cliques, and to maintain political positions through extensive patronage. Such practices, coupled with imperfect provisions to maintain the security of their own positions, brought down their regimes at the same time as they discredited their countries in the eyes of international investors.

28. Albert Fishlow, "Brazilian Size Distribution of Income," *American Economic Review* 62 (May 1972): 391–402; and Samuel A. Morley and Jeffrey G. Williamson, "The Impact of Demand on Labor Absorption and the Distribution of Earnings: The Case of Brazil" (Paper No. 39, Program of Development Studies, Rice University, Spring 1973). Mimeographed.

The contribution of the centralization-concentration-regressivity syndrome to economic growth may vary with several elements. One such element is the elite's use of the syndrome for public or private benefit. Another element is the capacity of the elite to keep the political system under control while it aggregates resources and makes crucial decisions on allocations. Related to this, perhaps, is the size of the population relative to the opportunities in traditional agriculture. When there is little population pressure—as in parts of Africa—the current regime may have breathing space in which to pursue growth through the central allocations of resources with relatively little concern for mass participation in the policy process. Another element may be the elite's cohesion. When the oligarchy is united in its support for its own political and economic prerogatives, there is less likelihood of mass protest engineered by disaffected members of the elite who look to populist politics as a way of strengthening their position.[29]

Still another factor may be the severity of deprivation experienced in the early stages of growth. Pre-1971 Pakistan presents a horrible example of how an elite should *not* distribute benefits and deprivations. Regime opponents could point to cultural, language, and regional isolation from the capital city, and to persistent economic deprivations, as mutually reinforcing justifications for civil war.[30]

Yet another element may be the current level of economic advancement. Those countries at the lowest levels of development may provide a setting for the centralization-concentration-regressivity syndrome to make its greatest contribution to development: a meager supply of educated personnel and a population likely to have little regard for public affairs, a low

29. See Robert E. Ward, "Political Modernization and Political Culture in Japan," in Claude E. Welch, Jr., *Political Modernization: A Reader in Comparative Political Change* (Belmont, Calif.: Duxbury, 1971).

30. See Rounaq Jahan, *Pakistan: Failure in National Integration* (New York: Columbia University Press, 1972).

sense of "political efficacy," and little awareness of events outside the local setting.[31] For countries at a slightly higher level of development, a number of factors may reduce the syndrome to an impediment rather than a stimulus for further development. Increases in popular education and political awareness may make the masses intolerant of the authoritarian leaders that had been supported by centralization and concentration. The greater supply of administrative manpower may render progressively distributed social services more feasible at the same time that greater political awareness creates demand for such services, and the spread of economic resources makes available a wider pool of revenue that can be tapped by progressive income taxes. In the least-developed nations, the syndrome of centralization-concentration-regressivity may produce the upper limits of its own usefulness to economic growth as the people's willingness to accept the short end of political and economic rewards erodes in the face of some upward change in their personal situations.

THE BRAZILIAN CASE

Brazil is currently one of the most thoroughly examined cases of rapid economic growth among the developing countries. It has attracted attention partly because the early period of the scenario—beginning in 1964—left the poorer classes with declining purchasing power, and partly because its "economic miracle" has been accompanied by a shift to authoritarian and repressive politics. As in Pakistan, whose spurt of economic growth in an earlier period also attracted much attention from Western economists but where the allocation of benefits went to a narrow social sector and laid the groundwork for a bloody civil war and the separation of Bangla Desh, the Brazilian experience prompts legitimate questions among those who think about economic growth: Can growth come without severe distortions in the distribution of benefits? And can it be

31. Adelman and Morris, *Society, Politics, and Economic Development.*

accomplished without harsh repressions being directed against those who object to the pattern of distribution?

The record of growth in the Brazilian economy is impressive: it reached more than 9 percent per year in real terms (i.e., after correcting for inflation) between 1968 and 1971.[32] For the working class, however, the record was an actual *decline* in real wages of some 20–25 percent between 1964 and 1967[33] and in some figures a decline of 64.5 percent between 1958 and 1969.[34] For the impoverished rural Northeast, the record shows declining fortunes relative to the industrial regions in the South.[35] As noted, a more recent study finds signs of a turnaround in the distribution of benefits to the low-income classes after these early deprivations.

Several analysts view the decline in real wages as a deliberate result of Brazilian strategy, which also included overt moves away from democratic government. The military figures in power since 1964, in this view, pursued rapid economic growth by a series of measures designed to encourage foreign investments and to promise lucrative rewards for Brazil's capitalists. They also moved sharply away from the open, democratic politics that marked the preceding years of the country's history and directed the tools of an increasingly powerful and sometimes brutal state against its opponents. Censorship of the mass media, arbitrary arrest, lengthy detention, and torture of political prisoners are among the charges widely leveled against the regime.[36]

32. Albert Fishlow, "Some Reflections on Post-1964 Brazilian Economic Policy," in *Authoritarian Brazil: Origins, Policies, and Future,* ed. Alfred Stepan (New Haven: Yale University Press, 1973), p. 69.

33. Thomas E. Skidmore, "Politics and Economic Policy Making in Authoritarian Brazil, 1937-71," in ibid., p. 20.

34. Philippe C. Schmitter, "The 'Portugalization' of Brazil?" in ibid., p. 200.

35. Fishlow, "Brazilian Economic Policy," p. 109.

36. Stepan, *Authoritarian Brazil.*

THE UNITED STATES EXPERIENCE

There should be some concern for the unpleasant dynamics of the Brazilian experience in the United States. Low-income states of this country are also marked by political traits of governmental centralization, political concentration, and strong executive leadership, plus the policy traits of regressive taxes and expenditures. Each of these has distinct analogies to Brazil. Yet, these similarities do not mean that economic growth here comes at great expense to the poor or threatens political liberties. Even in Brazil, there is some indication that the economic deprivations of the poor were only the *short-run* results of Brazilian growth policy. Moreover, wage earners in this country are better organized than those in most poor countries, and have demonstrated their capacity to guard their share of the growing national pie. For the lowest-income earners in the United States, most of them below the reach of the labor unions, there are protections in extensive social programs not available in most poor countries. If we look to the experience of the low-income states, we find growing income, political competition, and political participation all increasing more rapidly than the national trends. Table 6.1 shows representative data.

Again we see the benefits that accrue to the low-income sectors because the United States is a developed as well as a developing country. Affluence can invest in growth and at the same time attend to the needs of the poor. The resources to cushion the perils of economic growth are apparent in various parts of the national budget: community development and housing, education and manpower, health, income security, and veterans benefits and services. For fiscal year 1974, the national government spent $137.8 billion, or slightly more than 50 percent of its total outlay, on these programs. This is up from $35.7 billion and 30 percent of the total spent in 1965.[37]

37. The figures are taken from *The United States Budget in Brief, Fiscal Year 1975* (Washington, D.C.: U.S. Government Printing Office, 1974).

Table 6.1. **Personal Income, Party Competition, Voter Participation, Low-Income States* Relative to National Average, 1948–72**

	Income Per Capita	Percentage of Vote Won by Major Party in Race for Governor	Percentage of Voting-Age Population Casting Ballots in Contests for U.S. House of Representatives
1948 Low-income states** (a)	$ 952		29
National average (b)	1,329	NA	48
(a) as % of (b)	72%		60
1954 Low-income states** (a)	$1,164	76	37
National average (b)	1,637	61	57
(a) as % of (b)	71%	125	65
1960 Low-income states** (a)	$1,515	70	38
National average (b)	2,076	56	60
(a) as % of (b)	73%	125	63
1966 Low-income states** (a)	$2,161	63	44
National average (b)	2,784	56	56
(a) as % of (b)	78%	113	79
1972 Low-income states** (a)	$3,480	60	39
National average (b)	4,235	56	52
(a) as % of (b)	82%	107	75

* Ten states averaging lowest per capita personal income 1950–72: Alabama, Arkansas, Kentucky, Louisiana, Maine, Mississippi, North Carolina, South Carolina, Tennessee, West Virginia.
** Or within 1 or 2 years of date shown, depending on schedule of state elections.
Source: Statistical Abstracts of the United States (Washington, D.C.: U.S. Government Printing Office, 1950–73).

State and local governments add further sums to these programs. While not all the expenditures in these categories go to the "poor," the figures do illustrate the magnitude of resources available for social programs that train, provide health care, and assure at least minimum income security for low-income sectors of our population.

American Efforts in Regional Development

At times the great absolute wealth of the United States and the open political competition among groups seeking pieces of the economic pie lead to a proliferation of activities. The image of massive, but highly diffused resources appears in our recent experience with regional economic development.[38]

The topic of regional development recalls the Tennessee Valley Authority begun in the Great Depression and credited with saving the region from periodic flooding and stimulating economic development by providing extensive electric power. The model of regional growth received a new breath of life during the 1960s. Contributing factors were John Kennedy's campaign experience in West Virginia, which brought him face to face with dire poverty in the context of a primary campaign that proved crucial to his winning the Democratic nomination; and the widespread rediscovery of poverty by intellectual and political elites, partly through such books as Harry Caudill's *Night Comes to the Cumberlands.*

What started as a concern for the development of Appalachia, however, soon burgeoned into a surfeit of regional plans and a diffusion of resources. The concept of Appalachia itself escalated from the impoverished coal-mining counties of West Virginia and eastern Kentucky to include parts of thirteen states—from New York in the Northeast to Mississippi in

38. See Theodore J. Lowi, *The End of Liberalism* (New York: Norton, 1969).

the Southwest. By the time this grouping had been assembled—in large measure to increase the number of United States senators and representatives who would support the legislation—the area to be included encompassed almost 10 percent of the nation's population and was so diverse that mining was no longer a regionwide dominant source of employment! Further, incomes in the region were so diverse that Maryland's affected counties had an average per capita income more than twice that of Kentucky's.[39] Soon after, the regional theme spread further to include:

The Ozarks Regional Commission (parts of Arkansas, Oklahoma, Kansas, and Missouri)

The Four Corners Regional Commission (parts of Arizona, New Mexico, Colorado, and Utah)

The Coastal Plains Regional Commission (parts of Georgia, North Carolina, and South Carolina)

The Upper Great Lakes Regional Commission (parts of Michigan, Minnesota, and Wisconsin)

The New England Regional Commission (all of Connecticut, Maine, Massachusetts, New Hampshire, Rhode Island, and Vermont)[40]

Throughout this focus on regional development, a series of debates centered on how to proceed within the regional mode: Should aid be given to places or directly to individuals? Should the focus be on the development of the region's economy or the alleviation of poverty? Should there be incentives provided for the relocation of people or the relocation of jobs (i.e., should people move out of regions or should jobs move

39. Monroe Newman, *The Political Economy of Appalachia: A Case Study in Regional Integration* (Lexington, Mass.: Heath, 1972).

40. John H. Cumberland, *Regional Development Experiences and Prospects in the United States of America* (Paris: Mouton, 1971), p. 104.

in)? Should regional assistance be concentrated in the neediest areas or in areas most likely to develop or should assistance be dispersed to many sites? and How should regions be defined? [41] Just as the open and competitive political process took the regional idea and applied it to many parts of the country at the same time, so there were tendencies to answer questions in a multiplicity of ways. Resources were divided into many categories for many locales. After the programs had been in operation for several years and faced the need for legislative extension, the Nixon administration took the position that an excess of diffusion had contributed to a lack of clear success in the regional commissions. Yet the coalition of so many legislators (three-fifths of all United States senators had a stake in the measure) found the President's arguments unpersuasive. The regional commissions had their budgets continued but not significantly sharpened in their focus on specific targets.

Conclusions

This chapter has moved from a description of less-developed sectors within the United States to a frontal consideration of economic growth. It has faced certain challenges to the strategy of continued growth but finds that the challenges themselves encounter serious problems. True, the policy of growth provides no guarantees about its payoffs for the poor of a society. Under certain favorable conditions, however, growth may produce greater equality, perhaps after short-term deteriorations in the plight of the poorest and least-educated persons. Also, while growth promises no benign effects on the natural environment, techniques exist for minimizing the

41. Ibid., pp. 12–17.

threat to natural resources. Indeed, growth may be necessary to provide the resources to pay for the systematic conservation of nature. Poor countries, with real fears of hunger, seem unlikely to pay the high costs of controlling pollution or protecting the environment. For the developing sectors of the United States, however, national affluence should minimize the dangers that a strategy of growth presents either to the welfare of the poor or to the quality of the environment.

7

WHY SHOULD WE VIEW
THE UNITED STATES AS A
DEVELOPING COUNTRY?

There are several reasons for viewing the United States as a developing country. First, considerable poverty exists, whether measured by the number of people who fall below the government's "poverty line" conceived in annual income terms; by the continued existence of regional pockets like Appalachia that are both cultural and economic backwaters; by the social problems found in many urban areas; or by the presence of sizable racial and ethnic minorities whose levels of income, education, housing, and health fall noticeably below the norm for the population as a whole.

Second, related to poverty is the presence of dualism in the United States. As used in reference to the poor countries of Africa, Asia, and Latin America—and here in reference to the United States—dualism draws attention to the sharp contrasts between advanced and less-developed sectors that exist in close proximity to one another. For the poor countries, and for the United States, the sharpest and closest contrasts appear in the large cities: between steel-and-glass high-rise buildings or affluent residential neighborhoods on the one hand, and the physical squalor and social problems of the slums on the other. The United States shows greater economic contrasts between affluent and poor than any Western European country thought of as "developed." Moreover, the poverty that exists within the United States—also in contrast to that of other developed countries—is concentrated in minority racial groups, is increasingly urban in nature, and presents a tinderbox for severe conflict as in the burgeoning cities of many of the poor countries.

Third, the poor states of the United States show not only the poverty of low incomes, but also several features that have striking parallels with the politics of poor countries. Similarities include: dependence on outside sources of capital; local chafing at conditions imposed by outsiders; a prominent place for traditionalism in politics; governmental centralization; a concentration of political power in relatively few hands; a strong chief executive, often one who adds to his local stature by posturing against outside influences; and the pursuit of taxing and spending policies that distribute their burdens and benefits in a regressive way.

Fourth, the concern of political leaders in low-income states, central cities, and minority communities over further economic development is an additional parallel with the poor countries. Prominent signs of parallel drives for development include: the efforts of poor states to attract industry with public subsidies; statements of black respondents to opinion polls that show their primary concern with improved incomes, housing, and jobs; and the recognition by black citizens of those leaders identified with economic causes (e.g., Ralph Abernathy).

What Should We Do?

Perhaps the first thing is to recognize that this view of the United States as a developing country is only partially correct. The United States is also a developed country, usually scoring first among nations in that widely used indicator of economic well-being, income per capita. This recognition does not weaken our argument. Rather, the developed nature of the country provides the wherewithal for appropriate programs to aid those sectors making loud and legitimate demands for continued economic growth.

What are the proper responses to those demands for growth? It is beyond the mission of this book to produce many detailed recommendations for economic development. Nevertheless, perspectives developed in the previous chapters do suggest some general principles. They are, first, to recognize the depth and legitimacy of growth demands that come out of the relatively depressed sectors. Second, those who argue for the primacy of environmental conservation and/or the more equal distribution of benefits must also provide in their plans for those demanding growth.

What seems especially sad on the intellectual and political landscapes of the contemporary United States are those who fix their attentions on the most-developed sectors, exaggerate their importance in the whole, and offer sweeping prescriptions based on their knowledge of these enclaves. Daniel Bell's image of the postindustrial society is no more suitable for the United States of the 1970s than was his earlier vision of an "end of ideology," penned in the late 1950s before the rich explosions (intellectual and chemical) of ideologies in the 1960s. Only limited sectors of the United States are postindustrial, most typically those university towns where postindustrial writers dwell. Bell has overlooked prominent signs of poverty throughout the country. Some demands for industrialization coming from ghettos or from small towns suggest the presence of preindustrial economies. Also, Bell need travel only a few miles from the Harvard campus to see a cruel form of postindustrialism in Fall River, Massachusetts, and other New England cities, where industrial glory has departed and obsolescence is the prominent economic trait.

The fixation on limited growth—with or without a desire to distribute economic benefits more evenly—also seems shortsighted. Analyses of recent trends and projections into the future that lie behind such prescriptions make unrealistic assumptions. The most prominent item written in this genre, *The Limits to Growth,* curiously assumes no further changes in technology; in reality, the technological sector has shown rapid and continuous change, frequently enabling the production of more food, power, and other benefits from available sources. Thus, in contrast to the dire predictions contained within that and similar volumes, there seems little reason to expect resource depletion within the foreseeable future. The great problems standing in the way of material satisfactions are more likely to be political than physical. *The Limits to Growth* calls for drastic changes in human values and politics, but of an altruistic kind that seems unlikely to occur.

What are the chances for political elites and the public agreeing to more equal divisions of a fixed economic pie? It is not possible to assert with certainty what changes will or will not occur. The recent history of the United States has witnessed expansions in social programs designed to help the poor. At the same time, however, the money for many of these expansions has come from social security payroll taxes that weigh most heavily on wage earners in the lower- and lower-middle-income brackets.

In this country and elsewhere, benefits for the poor seem most likely to come in a setting where the wealthy also gain some direct benefits. This process is distasteful to many intellectuals inclined toward altruistic feelings. Ideas about benefits that "trickle down" and "feed the sparrows through the horses" have earned some scorn. Yet the promising route to more equal distributions of benefits seems to be through the path of economic growth: the affluent will receive tangible incentives for investing their capital and skills and the poor will benefit through more jobs and through more public resources to pay for such social programs as basic education, job training, income security, and efforts to upgrade housing, health care, and public recreation. To be sure, there is a bit of bribery in this process. In exchange for their own greater acquisitions, the well-to-do may accept greater distributions for the poor.

The alternative of forced redistribution through sharply progressive taxes and social programs appears to be impractical in the current political setting. Except for brief periods of national crisis like 1933–37 and 1964–66, which permitted extensive reforms in the progressive direction, the strongest political interests have favored only a moderate redistribution of benefits.[1] Moreover, our government's system of checks and balances offers an institutional setting that, most of the time, works against wholesale progressive reform. Recent years have seen considerable expansions of social programs, but there has also been more reliance on *regressive* forms of taxation to pay for these programs. Overall, there have not been overtly populist redistributions in the body politic. Table 7.1 shows changes in the twelve-year period following 1960. They have favored the generally regressive taxes on sales, property, and social security; these enjoyed a growth 63 percent more than that for the generally progressive taxes on personal and corporate incomes. In 1960, progressive taxes accounted for 10

1. See Frances Fox Piven and Richard A. Cloward, *Regulating the Poor: The Functions of Public Welfare* (New York: Vintage, 1971).

Table 7.1. **Government Revenues, by Source, 1960 and 1971-72**

	1960 (in millions)	1971-72 (in millions)	Percent change 1960 to 1971-72
Total national, state, and local government revenue	$153,102	$381,849	149.4
Individual and corporate income taxes	65,852 43.0%	146,556 38.5%	122.6
Taxes on sales, property, and Old Age, Survivors and Disability Insurance	51,513 33.6%	147,063 38.5%	185.5
Other revenue	35,737 23.3%	88,230 23.1%	146.9

Sources: Governmental Finances in 1971-72 and *Historical Statistics of Governmental Finances and Employment* (Washington, D.C.: U.S. Government Printing Office, 1973 and 1969).

percent more of total government revenues than regressive taxes. By 1971-72, however, regressive taxes had moved slightly ahead of the others in their proportion of the total.

The alternative of *revolutionary* redistribution of costs and benefits seems both unworkable in a practical sense and loathsome as a topic of serious consideration. The political base of revolutionaries in the United States is minuscule, the institutions of government are strong, and the historic record of the revolutionary prescription elsewhere is one of chaos and the frustration of noble purpose.

While the weight of this argument gives the edge to the

general principle of growth over the general principles of
conservatism or redistribution, nothing here endorses a growth
that is uncontrolled with respect to its consequences for the
environment or the distribution of its profits. This is not the
time to endorse laissez faire, caveat emptor, or the simplistic
form of *economic man*. In the United States more than in most
countries, the political process has been successful in for-
mulating and enforcing social goals to compete with sheer
growth. Indeed, the values of growth, conservatism, and equity
seem more compatible than contradictory. The coincidence of
a developed and developing sectors present complementary
resources and needs. Short of an effective and socially minded
authoritarianism, only a wealthy and dynamic economy can,
in any meaningful way, pursue such goals as an aesthetic
environment plus social and economic equity.

Can a Developing United States Offer Insights to Less-Developed Countries?

Throughout this study of the United States, we have relied on
writing about the developing countries. This has helped us to
see the dynamics of less-developed sectors in our own country,
and has sensitized us to their continued and legitimate pursuit
of economic growth. Recognizing their importance in our total
economic and political settings, we must qualify sharply any
notions about a postindustrial United States, or any policy that
would impose severe limits on further economic growth.

Can we turn around the analogy and find some relevance
in the experience of the United States for the less-developed
countries? This will be a detour from our basic concern to
improve our understanding about the United States. Nevertheless, a brief departure from our principal goal should,

at the least, sharpen our understanding of certain differences between the United States and the less-developed countries, and may go beyond that to stimulate some changes in thinking about the very poor countries.

It is not easy to provide a *brief* discussion of the poor countries. There are so many of them; they have such great variety in economics, culture, and politics. The vast majority of the United Nations fits into the categories of "less-developed" or "very poor." Geographically, the poor countries range from Spain, Greece, and Portugal in Europe to almost all the countries of Africa, Asia, and Latin America. The better-developed Latin American countries rank near the border of "better developed" and "less developed"; Asian countries follow; and African countries are the poorest. Significant exceptions in these patterns occur for Japan and Israel, which generally are considered economically developed, plus several oil-producing nations. Of course, all this depends on one's conception of economic development, as should be apparent in a book that treats the United States as a developing country.

There is almost as much variety in the writing about less-developed countries as in the countries themselves. Material differs on regional focus, topical interest, and political bias. Many anthropologists, economists, and historians have little to say about the points where culture, economics, politics, and public policy come together. Some of the literature carries a heavy burden of political ideology, viewing the poor countries as fit subjects for certain changes in their economics or politics or as cruelly exploited by governments and business firms based in Western Europe and North America. Like the missionaries who swarmed over the southern continents in an earlier age, some contemporary social scientists obscure a lot of reality in their efforts to do good.

Gunnar Myrdal's *Asian Drama: An Inquiry into the*

Poverty of Nations offers a useful treatment of complex issues. The book is limited, to be sure, by its focus on South Asia; but it identifies patterns that have been observed widely throughout the poor countries, and it deals with a set of issues—the mutual influence of economics, culture, and politics on policies toward economic development—that have special relevance for this book. Moreover, Myrdal writes sympathetically about the disadvantages that poor countries face in their international competitions with rich nations and multinational business firms, but he does not write with such a heavy ideology as to make a reader wary of his descriptions.

Myrdal identifies many impediments to rapid development that trouble the poor countries. These consist of their own cultural and political barriers to change, the serious nature of their economic problems, and their lack of competitive advantage with respect to the richer countries in international trade. Their cultural problems include local ideals that work against economic modernization: values respecting one's traditional loyalties to family and one's "place" in the occupations which—especially in the case of Hindu castes—are supported by religious norms and work against the freewheeling pursuit of an individual's economic opportunities in the manner of an unhindered Westerner. The easygoing character of life also serves to inhibit economic growth. The seemingly lethargic contentment of individuals with things as they are; and the infusion of this ideal into the apparatus of government which produces what Myrdal calls a "soft state," unable to enforce the regulations designed to guide investments and to modernize techniques in agriculture, local education, or public health. The soft state is not helped in its efforts to modernize the economy when it also faces other serious problems, e.g., demands for "nation-building" amid diverse languages and loyalties to ethnic groups, or a restive military.

Problems of culture and government in poor countries spill over into their economic sectors. Often there is a lack of an entrepreneurial class, or the entrepreneurial class that does exist lacks a legitimate status and must fight for its existence against the antagonism of cultural and governmental elites. Other economic problems result from the lack of rapport between professional economists oriented toward Western models of productivity but isolated from the indigenous groups whose cooperation is essential to make the plans work. A lack of rapport exists on each side of the wall: traditionalists who do not want to change and Western-oriented technocrats who are unable to adjust their visions to the local setting. Difficulties occur both for Western experts brought in to an indigenous setting and for local personnel removed from their roots by a Western-oriented education. In many ways the economy of the poor country is not ready for the simple translation of models derived in Europe or North America. In Myrdal's view, a most serious problem exists in the quality of the economic data available, which may consist of little more than poor guesses about the size of certain markets or the availability of certain skills.

Of course, the profound poverty of a region is another impediment to growth. Some areas are unable to lessen aggregate consumption for the purpose of accumulating investment capital without risking shortfalls in caloric intakes that will lessen human productivity. Population growth may keep ahead of marginal increases in output and further stifle the hoped-for multiplication of output through savings and investment in additional capacity. Some efforts designed to foster growth actually trigger events that are counterproductive: irrigation schemes needed to increase agricultural productivity via hybrid seeds may leech valuable minerals from the soil; the same schemes may require the consolidation of peasant holdings for more efficient production but, in the process, force people from the land and to the cities without any preparation for urban employment; and an increase in the regulatory capacity of government may foster more corruption as existing economic interests seek to buy their way around the procedures designed to guide economic development.

Myrdal also points to the international problems of very poor countries. They must deal with rich nations that both supply technologies and equipment needed for economic growth and purchase raw materials or simple manufactures from the poor countries. Typically there are more suppliers of raw materials or simple manufactures than of the sophisticated machinery; especially when the poor country depends on out-siders for extracting and processing their resources (because of the shortages in local talent and capital), they are likely to suffer the smallest profit in the exchange and thus have few resources available to invest in subsequent development.

One of the ironies that works against poor countries is their arrival as "sovereign" nations after the period of colonialism. There is little possibility for presently developing countries to repeat the European experience of the nineteenth century, i.e., to exploit peoples in even more backward areas who would serve as captive sources of supplies or markets. Further, economic growth now depends on industrial plants that are more complex and expensive than those which prevailed at the economic "takeoff" in Europe and North America. The need to import capital-intensive equipment to become competitive in world markets not only frustrates the other needs of many poor countries to absorb surplus man-power, but also imposes severe costs in terms of hard currency. Numerous poor countries face:

> a negative balance of payments already inherent in the lagging export demands and the increased food needs consequent upon the population explosion. This gap

between import needs and export possibilities has been widening and is bound to widen further. While the obvious remedy is capital inflow to cover the deficits and enable the . . . countries to import essentials for consumption and the capital goods necessary in furthering import substitution, the deterioration in their trading position is itself likely to decrease the availability of foreign capital.[2]

John Kenneth Galbraith's book *Economics and the Public Purpose* sheds additional light on the international disadvantages of poor countries.[3] Galbraith writes about the multinational business firms that have come to dominate commerce since World War II. Galbraith is not the first economist to discover these firms. Other writers, too, have described their size, showing several of these firms to be larger in economic scale than many countries of the world. If General Motors were a country, it would rank as the twenty-third largest in terms of its annual product, just ahead of Switzerland; Standard Oil of New Jersey would rank twenty-seventh; and the Ford Motor Company twenty-ninth.[4] Countries—especially poor countries—have serious problems in regulating these firms which do business in so many places that they effectively escape the regulation of any public bodies.[5]

Galbraith's discussion of these huge firms is useful for showing their influences on the problems both of the poor

2. Gunnar Myrdal, *An Approach to the Asian Drama* (Selections from *Asian Drama: An Inquiry into the Poverty of Nations*) (New York: Vintage, 1970), p. 151.
3. John Kenneth Galbraith, *Economics and the Public Purpose* (Boston: Houghton Mifflin, 1973).
4. Lester R. Brown, *World Without Borders* (New York: Vintage, 1972), pp. 214–15.
5. See, for example, Robert O. Keohane and Joseph S. Nye, Jr., eds., "Transnational Relations and World Politics," *International Organization* 25 (Summer 1971); and Lester R. Brown, *World Without Borders.*

countries and the poor sectors of the United States. He shows us another side of the United States as a developing country.

The power of the large multinational firms, in Galbraith's view, reflects their superior position with respect to market forces. They make and implement decisions about investments, product development, and sales not so much according to the market's play of supply and demand, but in response to their own planning system. Firms with huge size and virtual monopolies over the technologies required in their sector can decide about products and prices, and pretty much control the buying of inputs and the selling of products. Many of their transactions involve governments; and their importance as armaments suppliers, employers of numerous persons, and consumers of vast supplies involving the fortunes of numerous other companies ensures the cooperation of public bodies in setting favorable economic conditions. When they come to dealing with the public, these firms control product design along with their few "competitors," and affect public demands via mass advertising.

Part of the planning of large firms entails close relations with the suppliers of labor. This encourages the development of large unions with powerful leaders, capable of winning generous terms for their members. The employees of large firms are relatively well off, but the combination of large firms and large unions adds to the upward spiral of inflation. There is, in effect, no market mechanism linking the firms with labor that would compensate for an oversupply of labor with deflationary wage changes. Galbraith writes that corporate managers look after their own salary needs and those of labor, and give secondary concern to shareholders' profit and to the general public's interest in stable costs. For the American economy, where most of these large firms are based, this produces a two-tiered structure. On top are planning-system firms, aided by government in obtaining capital, whose employees are on the leading edge of inflation and able to resist its inroads. On the bottom are lower-paid employees of firms still heavily dependent on market forces for their supplies of capital and labor, and for selling their goods.

Like others who have written about multinational firms, Galbraith notes their great clout in the poor countries. A poor country may need a firm's products more than the firm needs the raw material or market in the poor country. At home, the firms have learned to deal with government instead of depending on market forces; in the somewhat different terrain of poor countries these firms deal with governments in the appropriate way. Often this means extraordinary payoffs to key officials who provide the market protections desired or facilitate unusual rates of return to justify the firm's investments in "unstable" areas; this leaves to the poor economies the need to pay heavily for the firm's products in hard currency, or in the opportunities foregone to develop the indigenous skills.

An outsider finds it difficult to avoid pessimism about the prospects of poor countries for rapid economic development. Not only is there pervasive poverty along with continued population growth, keeping people at the brink of subsistence, but also cultural and political traits that are not conducive to economic development amid severe competitive disadvantages internationally. Lacking is any substantial international altruism, or viable institutions that can tax wealthy nations to aid poor nations. Poor countries lack the access to the pocketbooks of the wealthy that has served—through intergovernmental transfers—to improve materially the economies of poor states within the United States.

The dynamics of sharp increases in the price of petroleum during 1973–74 show the Hobbesian nature of international economics. When the oil-producing countries discovered their capacity for unity, they mandated take-it-or-leave-it price increases. Many oil importers protested, but the greatest burdens rested on the very poor countries. Originally it was the United States and other potential supporters of Israel that were the targets of the oil embargo. As the embargo turned into price increases, however, the industrial powers found they could pay the new cost of petroleum, albeit with difficulty, and could reexport some of the increase as part of the inflation built into the prices of their manufactured goods. For the very poor countries with simple economies, this meant increases in the price of goods manufactured in Europe, Japan, and North America as well as the direct increase in oil prices. At an early point in the price hikes, the oil producers spoke of a development fund to ease the burdens on the poor countries. More than a year into the new prices, however, that proposal seems far from alleviating any real hardships. The oil producers have learned they can hold together to demand higher prices, and even though many of them are having great difficulty absorbing their new revenues, the "me first" character of international economics offers no incentives for a price rollback.

The amount of resources transferred in international aid is tiny compared to what is available from one sector of the United States to another. Consider the increases in national government aid to American states and localities from 1960 to 1973. In per capita terms in 1967 dollars, eliminating the effect of inflation, the growth was from $44.10 to $161.98, and from 13.5 to 23.5 percent of state and local budgets. In the midst of this period, an estimate of the aid funds available to an average developing country was some $1.00 to $2.00 per capita per year.[6]

From 1967 to 1972, United States foreign grants and credits showed an increase from $6.7 billion to $8.0 billion in current dollars. However, these programs suffered a decline as

6. Robert B. Bangs, *Financing Economic Development: Fiscal Policy for Emerging Countries* (Chicago: University of Chicago Press, 1968), pp. 83–88.

percentages of total United States government expenditures: from 4.2 to 3.4. And in real dollars—correcting for inflation—there was a decline of 4.5 percent.[7] One message of this book is that our own domestic efforts to smooth the differences between rich and poor sectors have been something less than a complete success. The greater diversity of national interests throughout the world, and the lack of a meaningful international sovereign capable of redistributing resources, bodes even less well for the poor countries than for the poor of the United States.

This pessimism about the future of poor countries does not project frozen levels of development. While the cards seemed stacked against rapid or dramatic economic development, there are prospects for *some improvements*. Great variety exists between the poor countries, and great diversity within many of them. Small and segmental victories against poverty or lethargy are worth something, both for the productivity they offer and for the demonstration that effort is worth something. Many people who have worked in poor countries tell stories of success and bright prospects. Some speak of indigenous people trained in Western techniques, who seem to have the assertiveness to resist local pressures against their developmental aspirations as well as the intelligence to blend a sensitive recognition of local potential along with goals derived in a foreign setting. Certain agricultural and industrial projects are working not only to pay the costs of their investments but to produce surpluses for subsequent investments. Travelers who passed through cities like Taipei or Bangkok only a few years apart have noted the signs of economic development in changed modes of transport: from foot, animal, and pedicab—through the bicycle and motorcycle periods—and right on to the private motorcar. As noted in chapter 4, *favelas* around

7. *Statistical Abstract of the United States, 1973* (Washington, D.C.: U.S. Government Printing Office, 1974), p. 770.

the capital cities of poor countries are not always the stagnant slums of first appearance: they reflect some upward dynamism in the movement of peasants to the city in search for better economic opportunities, and they may include stable family structures and physical structures that improve with the families' first success in the urban economy.

One of the promising themes in the writing about poor countries urges Western experts to be humble in their efforts to study and guide development. Several grand efforts by outsiders have not succeeded in remaking indigenous cultures, economies, and politics. The Alliance for Progress was much less of a success than Project Apollo, whose aspiration to put men on the moon proved simpler than the aspirations of the same period to change foreign cultures. Albert O. Hirschman has acquired an international reputation for: his skeptical questioning of grand designs; his suggestions to work on smaller, more manageable segments in the economies of poor countries; and his willingness to rely on the people of those countries to take advantage of the stimuli provided by relatively simple inputs.[8]

Again, and Finally, the United States

For the plight of the less-developed sectors of the United States, we may apply some of the lessons acquired from developmental efforts in the poor countries. The economics and cultures of our poor states, urban enclaves, and black nation are complex; and they resist detailed management from central authorities who aspire to dramatic change. Our government has access to far more skilled personnel and

8. See Albert O. Hirschman, *The Strategy for Economic Development* (New Haven: Yale University Press, 1958), and *Journeys Toward Progress: Studies of Economic Policy-Making in Latin America* (New York: Norton, 1973).

financial capital than governments of the poor countries, and we have seen considerable progress across a wide range of economic and social indicators. Yet we have also bungled our share of reforms that have proved too simplistic for the subtleties of the needs. The complete ban on DDT may be a case in point, conceived as necessary to save wildlife and humans, but enacted at a high cost in terms of disease outbreak and the costly and sometimes deadly nature of substitutes used for the control of agricultural pests.[9] Our government as well as those of poor countries can work with a heavy hand, whether motivated by "good" or "bad" interests.

The tasks of major reform in providing more opportunities to the less-developed sectors of the United States—and more so the world—are truly formidable. The recent surge of inflation and unemployment cannot help but make the task more difficult. With poor families using a higher percentage of their incomes for necessary consumption, they pay a more severe price for inflation in a lowered standard of living than upper-income families. American foundations, including Ford, Rockefeller, and Danforth, have cut back on their social programs in the face of deteriorating stock-market portfolios. And in the face of hardships at home and price squeezes from Arab oil producers, the United States Congress seems in little mood to increase our foreign aid for humanitarian projects. The sharp inflation and unemployment may set back recent progress in narrowing the gap between developing and developed sectors. How much setback occurs may depend on how long and how steep are the spurts of inflation and unemployment. These are serious problems that harden several issues addressed in this book. But they should not cause us to overlook what may be the more lasting issue: that involving

9. See Rita Gray Beatty, *The DDT Myth: Triumph of the Amateurs* (New York: John Day, 1973).

the alternatives of growth and conservation, and how much of aggregate resources should be devoted to each.

In the face of serious economic problems, it is tempting to opt for simple political solutions. It may be especially tempting for an economist, hopeful that things are easier across the street in the terrain of another social science. Thus, John Kenneth Galbraith proposes a beefing-up of the staff assistance available to the United States Congress, and assuring public hearings as part of congressional committee deliberations. About the public hearings, he writes:

> These would provide occasion for full expression of individual and organized views as to the proper allocation of public resources. . . . This would have an immediate effect in guiding congressional decision; it would have the more important consequence of making the allocation of resources a public issue.[10]

In Galbraith's view, these reforms of the legislative branch (which he sees as naturally more inclined to aid smaller economic interests than is the executive branch) would lead to more support for market-determined transactions and lessen the dominance of firms that can plan their price and product policies with government support. For our purposes, the reform would lessen the centralized control of the economy and might free more resources for the use of less-developed sectors. Yet the route between these political reforms and economic change appears to be long and questionable. Ours is a government with multiple checks and balances. Interests (i.e., large firms) losing a battle in one arena still have other lines of defense to hold back an adverse change in economic policy. This is not to say that continued progress toward equalizing economic distributions is impossible. It is to say,

10. Galbraith, *Economics and Public Purpose,* p. 300.

however, that there is little probable success in an effort to deceive powerful interests through a sharp change in government structure.

When all is said, however, the prime task of this book is analysis, falling short of prescription. Or, to put it more correctly, the key prescription pertains to proper modes of analysis. It is this: look with skepticism at the writings about postindustrialism in the United States and limits to growth, and recognize the deeply rooted and legitimate demands for continued economic growth that come from those sectors in the United States that give it the appearance of a developing country. Those who would react to this prescription and proceed to plan for economic growth need not ignore all that is written in works concerned with limited growth. As a developed as well as a developing country, the United States has resources to spend on pollution control and social programs even while it encourages further growth. It is neither necessary nor appropriate to ignore the demands for growth and concentrate only on conservation; or to hope for political changes that will divide a fixed economic pie into equal pieces.

INDEX

183